Milwaukee Brewers 2019

A Baseball Companion

Edited by Patrick Dubuque, Aaron Gleeman and Bret Sayre

Baseball Prospectus

Craig Brown and Dave Pease, Consultant Editors
Rob McQuown and Harry Pavlidis, Statistics Editors

Copyright © 2019 by DIY Baseball, LLC.
All rights reserved

This book or any part thereof may not be reproduced or transmitted in any form or by any means, electronic or mechanical, including photocopying, recording, or by any information storage and retrieval system, without permission in writing from the publisher.

Limit of Liability/Disclaimer of Warranty: While the publisher and the author have used their best efforts in preparing this book, they make no representations or warranties with respect to the accuracy or completeness of the contents of this book and specifically disclaim any implied warranties of merchantability or fitness for a particular purpose. No warranty may be created or extended by sales representatives or written sales materials. The advice and strategies contained herein may not be suitable for your situation. You should consult with a professional where appropriate. Neither the publisher nor the author shall be liable for any loss of profit or any other commercial damages, including but not limited to special, incidental, consequential, or other damages.

Library of Congress Cataloging-in-Publication Data:
paperback
ISBN-13: 978-1-949332-44-5

Project Credits
Cover Design: Kathleen Dyson
Interior Design and Production: Jeff Pease, Dave Pease
Layout: Jeff Pease, Dave Pease

Baseball icon courtesy of Uberux, from https://www.shareicon.net/author/uberux

Ballpark diagram courtesy of Lou Spirito/THIRTY81 Project, https://thirty81project.com/

Manufactured in the United States of America
10 9 8 7 6 5 4 3 2 1

Table of Contents

Foreword v
    Rob Mains

Statistical Introduction vii

Part 1: Team Analysis

Table for Three: Previewing the 2019 Milwaukee Brewers 3
    J.P. Breen, Paul Noonan and Sean Roberts

Performance Graphs 9

2018 Team Performance 10

2019 Team Projections 11

Team Personnel 12

Miller Park Stats 13

Brewers Team Analysis 15

Part 2: Player Analysis

Brewers Player Analysis 20

Brewers Prospects 99

Part 3: Featured Articles

The Hole in The Shift is Fixing Itself 109
    Russell Carleton

The State of the Quality Start 113
    Rob Mains

Heads-Up Hacking—The First Pitch 119
    Matthew Trueblood

A Hymn for the Index Stat 125
    Patrick Dubuque

Index of Names 129

Foreword

Rob Mains

Welcome to this companion of the 2019 Milwaukee Brewers. We at Baseball Prospectus are excited to provide this analysis of the Brewers.

Our website, Baseball Prospectus, is a leader in delivering high-quality commentary and data to baseball fans everywhere. To some, those words—commentary and data—appear mutually exclusive. There are people out there who believe that traditional analysis and advanced analytics must run on different paths. But the simplistic narrative of stats vs. traditionalists just isn't true. Every team's analytics department interacts with scouting, development, and major league operations with a common goal: Delivering a championship. New technologies, like radar tracking of pitch speeds and movement, enable talent evaluators to focus on qualitative aspects of pitching like mechanics and pitch sequencing. In-game strategies like infield shifts, based on batters' hit tendencies, help turn balls in play into outs. Hitters use information to adjust their swings to maximize run production.

All these numbers can seem, at best, intimidating, and at worst, counterproductive to the casual fan. Even as technology and analysis have embedded themselves deeply into the way teams run, it can often feel like statistics create a displacement between the viewer and the sport, breaking them out of the action. And yet every fan incorporates the numbers to some degree; stats like batting average and earned run average, so fundamental to how we talk about performance, are actually complicated formulas. They don't bother people because those formulas have become second nature, as easy to translate as the action on the field.

Along the way, new statistics have entered baseball's lexicon. You'll see some of them, like on-base percentage (which measures a batter's ability to get on base via walk, hit batter, or hit), OPS (on-base plus slugging), and average exit velocity (the speed of balls off a hitter's bat) on broadcasts. Others, like DRC+, might well be new to you. Some of them have been well-defined to the public, others haven't. That lack of context has created ambiguity. Fans know that a ball hit 100 mph is scorched, but does that mean extra bases? (Not if it's hit on the ground or high in the air it doesn't.)

For those who are amenable to them, the new statistics can increase the enjoyment and understanding of the game. They can help fans identify when a pitcher is tiring, when a stolen base or a bunt attempt makes sense (and, more often, when it doesn't), or how a team's lineup might be constructed. Websites like Baseball Prospectus add to that understanding by weaving metrics into the narrative of the game. That's the goal of this publication: to take some of the newer, more complicated statistics and make them as intuitive as the ones on the back of old baseball cards.

But you don't need to love analytics to love baseball. The fans at BP who worked together to write this guide are captivated first and foremost by the game itself. We're drawn to Aaron Judge's power, Francisco Lindor's glove, Billy Hamilton's speed and Patrick Corbin's slider and don't need numbers to tell us why they're so mesmerizing. The underlying statistics provide depth to the game that we all love.

We hope you'll find that this guide helps you better understand the Brewers. Our analysts have studied the team's major league personnel and its minor league affiliates to identify their strengths and weaknesses, both the obvious ones and those that only a careful dissection of players' performances—yes, including the data—can reveal. You don't need us to tell you who was good and who wasn't in 2018, but our models and writers can help you project how each player is going to perform this year and beyond, and appreciate the greatness of each new game as it unfolds. As in the sport itself, the human and analytic components combine to generate a deeper overall understanding.

Think back to the first time you saw a baseball game on a high-definition TV. You'd grown familiar with how the game looked and felt on a picture tube. But new TV allowed you to see details that you'd never seen before. That's how advanced statistics work. The game itself is why you're here and why you're buying this. (And, for that matter, why we wrote it.) The statistical measures provide the sharper focus, the detail, the depth of knowledge that you didn't have before, generating an overall superior picture. Enjoy the view.

—*Rob Mains is an author of Baseball Prospectus.*

Statistical Introduction

Sports are, fundamentally, a blend of athletic endeavor and storytelling. Baseball, like any other sport, tells its stories in so many ways: in the arc of a game from the stands or a season from the box scores, in photos, or even in numbers. At Baseball Prospectus, we understand that statistics don't replace observation or any of baseball's stories, but complement everything else that makes the game so much fun.

What stats help us with is with patterns and precision, variance and value. This book can help you learn things you may not see from watching a game or hundred, whether it's the path of a career over time or the breadth of the entire MLB. We'd also never ask you to choose between our numbers and the experience of viewing a game from the cheap seats or the comfort of your home; our publication combines running the numbers with observations and wisdom from some of the brightest minds we can find. But if you *do* want to learn more about the numbers beyond what's on the backs of player jerseys, let us help explain.

Offense

At the end of this past year, we've revised our methodology for determining batting value. Long-time readers of Baseball Prospectus will notice that we've retired True Average in favor of a new metric: Deserved Runs Created Plus (DRC+). Developed by Jonathan Judge and our stats team, this statistic measures everything a player does at the plate–reaching base, hitting for power, making outs, and moving runners over–and puts it on a scale where 100 equals league-average performance. A DRC+ of 150 is terrific, a DRC+ of 100 is average, and a DRC+ of 75 means you better be an excellent defender.

DRC+ also does a better job than any of our previous metrics in taking contextual factors into account. The model adjusts for how the park affects performance, but also for things like the talent of the opposing pitcher, value of different types of batted-ball events, league, temperature, and other factors. It's able to describe a player's expected offensive contribution than any other statistic we've found over the years, and also does a better job of predicting future performance as well.

The other aspect of run-scoring is baserunning, which we quantify using Baserunning Runs. BRR not only records the value of stolen bases (or getting caught in the act), but also accounts for a runner's ability to go first to third on a single or advance on a fly ball.

Defense

Where offensive value is *relatively* easy to identify and understand, defensive value is ... not. Over the past dozen years, the sabermetric community has focused mostly on stats based on zone data: a real-live human person records the type of batted ball and estimated landing location, and models are created that give expected outs. From there, you can compare fielders' actual outs to those expected ones. Simple, right?

Unfortunately, zone data has two major issues. First, zone data is recorded by commercial data providers who keep the raw data private unless you pay for it. (All the statistics we build in this book and on our website use public data as inputs.) That hurts our ability to test assumptions or duplicate results. Second, over the years it has become apparent that there's quite a bit of "noise" in zone-based fielding analysis. Sometimes the conclusions drawn from zone data don't hold up to scrutiny, and sometimes the different data provided by different providers don't look anything alike, giving wildly different results. Sometimes the hard-working professional stringers or scorers might unknowingly inflict unconscious bias into the mix: for example good fielders will often be credited with more expected outs despite the data, and ballparks with high press boxes tend to score more line drives than ones with a lower press box.

Enter our Fielding Runs Above Average (FRAA). For most positions, FRAA is built from play-by-play data, which allows us to avoid the subjectivity found in many other fielding metrics. The idea is this: count how many fielding plays are made by a given player and compare that to expected plays for an average fielder at their position (based on pitcher ground-ball tendencies and batter handedness). Then we adjust for park and base-out situations.

When it comes to catchers, our methodology is a little different thanks to the laundry list of responsibilities they're tasked with beyond just, well, catching and throwing the ball. By now you've probably heard about "framing" or the art of making umpires more likely to call balls outside the strike zone for strikes. To put this into one tidy number, we incorporate pitch tracking data (for the years it exists) and adjust for important factors like pitcher, umpire, batter, and home-field advantage using a mixed-model approach. This grants us a number for how many strikes the catcher is personally adding to (or subtracting from) his pitchers' performance ... which we then convert to runs added or lost using linear weights.

Framing is one of the biggest parts of determining catcher value, but we also take into account blocking balls from going past, whether a scorer deems it a passed ball or a wild pitch. We use a similar approach–one that really benefits from the pitch tracking data that tells us what ends up in the dirt and what doesn't. We also include a catcher's ability to prevent stolen bases and how well they field balls in play, and *finally* we come up with our FRAA for catchers.

Pitching

Both pitching and fielding make up the half of baseball that isn't run scoring: run prevention. Separating pitching from fielding is a tough task, and most recent pitching analysis has branched off from Voros McCracken's famous (and controversial) statement, "There is little if any difference among major-league pitchers in their ability to prevent hits on balls hit in the field of play." The research of the analytic community has validated this to some extent, and there are a host of "defense-independent" pitching measures that have been developed to try and extricate the effect of the defense behind a hurler from the pitcher's work.

Our solution to this quandary is Deserved Run Average (DRA), our core pitching metric. DRA looks like earned run average (ERA), the tried-and-true pitching stat you've seen on every baseball broadcast or box score from the past century, but it's very different. To start, DRA takes an event-by-event look at what the pitchers does, and adjusts the value of that event based on different environmental factors like park, batter, catcher, umpire, base-out situation, run differential, inning, defense, home field advantage, pitcher role, and temperature. That mixed model gives us a pitcher's expected contribution, similar to what we do for our DRC+ model for hitters and FRAA model for catchers. (Oh, and we also consider the pitcher's effect on basestealing and on balls getting past the catcher.)

It's important to note that DRA is set to the scale of runs allowed per nine innings (RA9) instead of ERA, which makes DRA's scale slightly higher than ERA's. The reason for this is because ERA tends to overrate three types of pitchers:

1. Pitchers who play in parks where scorers hand out more errors. Official scorers differ significantly in the frequency at which they assign errors to fielders.
2. Ground-ball pitchers, because a substantial proportion of errors occur on grounders.
3. Pitchers who aren't very good. Better pitchers often allow fewer unearned runs than bad pitchers, because good pitchers tend to find ways to get out of jams.

Since the last time you picked up an edition of this book, we've also made a few minor changes to DRA to make it better. Recent research into "tunneling"–the act of throwing consecutive pitches that appear similar from a batter's point of view until after the swing decision point–data has given us a new contextual factor to account for in DRA: plate distance. This refers to the distance between successive pitches as they approach the plate, and while it has a smaller effect than factors like velocity or whiff rate, it still can help explain pitcher strikeout rate in our model.

New Pitching Metrics for 2019

We're including a few "new" pitching metrics for 2019's suite of Baseball Prospectus publications, but you may be familiar with them if you've spent time scouring the internet for stats.

Fastball Percentage

Our fastball percentage (FB%) statistic measures how frequently a pitcher throws a pitch classified as a "fastball," measured as a percentage of overall pitches thrown. We qualify three types of fastballs:

1. The traditional four-seam fastball;
2. The two-seam fastball or sinker;
3. "Hard cutters," which are pitches that have the movement profile of a cut fastball and are used as the pitcher's primary offering or in place of a more traditional fastball.

For example, a pitcher with a FB% of 67 throws any combination of these three pitches about two-thirds of the time.

Whiff Rate

Everybody loves a swing and a miss, and whiff rate (WHF) measures how frequently pitchers induce a swinging strike. To calculate WHF, we add up all the pitches thrown that ended with a swinging strike, then divide that number by a pitcher's total pitches thrown. Most often, high whiff rates correlate with high strikeout rates (and overall effective pitcher performance).

Called Strike Probability

Called Strike Probability (CSP) is a number that represents the likelihood that all of a pitcher's pitches will be called a strike while controlling for location, pitcher and batter handedness, umpire and count. Here's how it works: on each pitch, our model determines how many times (out of 100) that a similar pitch was called for a strike given those factors mentioned above, and when normalized for each batter's strike zone. Then we average the CSP for all pitches thrown by a pitcher in a season, and that gives us the yearly CSP percentage you see in the stats boxes.

As you might imagine, pitchers with a higher CSP are more likely to work in the zone, where pitchers with a lower CSP are likely locating their pitches outside the normal strike zone, for better or for worse.

Projections

Many of you aren't turning to this book just for a look at what a player has done, but for a look at what a player is going to do: the PECOTA projections. PECOTA, initially developed by Nate Silver (who has moved on to greater fame as a political analyst), consists of three parts:

1. Major-league equivalencies, which use minor-league statistics to project how a player will perform in the major leagues;
2. Baseline forecasts, which use weighted averages and regression to the mean to estimate a player's current true talent level; and
3. Aging curves, which uses the career paths of comparable players to estimate how a player's statistics are likely to change over time.

With all those important things covered, let's take a look at what's in the book this year.

Team Prospectus

You bought this book to learn more about your favorite (or maybe least-favorite, who are we to judge?) team, so let's talk about them. After a thoughtful preview of the 2019 season, you'll be presented with our Team Prospectus. This outlines many of the key statistics for each team's 2018 season, as well as a very inviting stadium diagram.

First you'll find the Performance Graphs page. The first is the 2018 Hit List Ranking. This shows our Hit List Rank for the team on each day of the 2018 season and is intended to give you a picture of the ups and downs of the team's season, including their highest and lowest ranks of the year. Hit List Rank measures overall team performance and drives the Hit List Power Rankings at the baseballprospectus.com website.

The second graph is Committed Payroll and helps you see how the team's payroll has compared to the MLB and divisional average payrolls over time. Payroll figures are currents as of January 1, 2019; with so many free agents still unsigned as of this writing, the final 2018 figure will likely be significantly different for many teams. (In the meantime, you can always find the most current data at Baseball Prospectus' Cot's Baseball Contracts page.)

The third graph is Farm System Ranking and displays how the Baseball Prospectus prospect team has ranked the organization's farm system since 2007. It also indicates the highest and lowest ranks that the farm system achieved over that time.

We start the Team Performance page with the squad's unadjusted and third-order 2018 win-loss records, presented in divisional context. We then list the three highest performing hitters and pitchers by WARP for 2018. Beneath that are a host of other team statistics. **Pythag** presents an adjusted 2018 winning percentage, calculated by taking runs scored per game (**RS/G**) and runs allowed per game (**RA/G**) for the team, and running them through a version of Bill James' Pythagorean formula that was refined and improved by David Smyth and Brandon Heipp. (The formula is called "Pythagenpat," which is equally fun to type and to say.)

Next up is **DRC+**, described earlier, to indicate the overall hitting ability of the team either above or below league-average. Run prevention on the pitching side is covered by **DRA** (also mentioned earlier) and another metric: Fielding Independent Pitching (**FIP**), which calculates another ERA-like statistic based on strikeouts, walks, and home runs recorded. Defensive Efficiency Rating (**DER**) tells us the percentage of balls in play turned into outs for the team, and is a quick fielding shorthand that rounds out run prevention.

After that, we have several measures related to roster composition, as opposed to on-field performance. **B-Age** and **P-Age** tell us the average age of a team's batters and pitchers, respectively. **Salary** is the combined team payroll for all on-field players, and Doug Pappas' Marginal Dollars per Marginal Win (**M$/MW**) tells us how much money a team spent to earn production above replacement level.

Ending this batch of statistics is the number of disabled list days a team had over the season (**DL Days**) and the amount of salary paid to players on the disabled list (**$ on DL**); this final number is expressed as a percentage of total payroll.

Next to each of these stats, we've listed each team's MLB rank in that category from 1st to 30th. In this, 1st always indicates a positive outcome and 30th a negative outcome, except in the case of salary–1st is highest.

The Team Projections page is intended to convey the team's operational capacity entering the 2019 season. We start with the team's PECOTA projected record for 2019, again in divisional context. The **+/-** column indicates how many more or less wins the team is projected to get than they got in 2018. We then list the three highest projected hitters and pitchers by WARP for 2018. A brief farm system summary follows, with the team's top prospect and number of BP Top 101 Prospects. Finally, we list the key new players and departed players, along with their 2019 projected WARP.

www.baseballprospectus.com

Alex Bregman 3B

Born: 03/30/94 Age: 25 Bats: R Throws: R
Height: 6'0" Weight: 180 Origin: Round 1, 2015 Draft (#2 overall)

YEAR	TEAM	LVL	AGE	PA	R	2B	3B	HR	RBI	BB	K	SB	CS	AVG/OBP/SLG
2016	CCH	AA	22	285	54	16	2	14	46	42	26	5	3	.297/.415/.559
2016	FRE	AAA	22	83	17	6	0	6	15	5	12	2	1	.333/.373/.641
2016	HOU	MLB	22	217	31	13	3	8	34	15	52	2	0	.264/.313/.478
2017	HOU	MLB	23	626	88	39	5	19	71	55	97	17	5	.284/.352/.475
2018	HOU	MLB	24	705	105	51	1	31	103	96	85	10	4	.286/.394/.532
2019	HOU	MLB	25	675	96	38	3	23	78	73	107	12	4	.272/.359/.463

Breakout: 6% Improve: 52% Collapse: 5% Attrition: 2% MLB: 100%
Comparables: Anthony Rendon, David Wright, Pablo Sandoval

YEAR	TEAM	LVL	AGE	PA	DRC+	VORP	BABIP	BRR	FRAA	WARP
2016	CCH	AA	22	285	172	38.9	.286	1.6	SS(51): -3.4, 3B(11): 1.4	2.7
2016	FRE	AAA	22	83	161	10.0	.333	-1.2	SS(14): 2.1, LF(3): -0.1	0.8
2016	HOU	MLB	22	217	107	9.6	.317	0.5	3B(40): 0.9, SS(6): -0.1	1.1
2017	HOU	MLB	23	626	114	34.7	.311	-1.5	3B(132): 8.7, SS(30): -2.9	3.9
2018	HOU	MLB	24	705	150	72.6	.289	-1.6	3B(136): 5.4, SS(28): -0.4	7.4
2019	HOU	MLB	25	675	125	37.3	.295	0.0	3B 7, SS 0	4.6

After the projections page, we share a few items about the team's home ballpark. There's the aforementioned diagram of the park's dimensions (including distances to the outfield wall), a few important biographical facts about the stadium, a graphic showing the height of the wall from the left-field pole to the right-field pole, and a table showing three-year park factors for the stadium. The park factors are displayed as indexes where 100 is average, 110 means that the park inflates the statistic in question by 10 percent, and 90 means that the park deflates the statistic in question by 10 percent.

Following the ballpark page, we have a **Personnel** section that lists many of the important decision-makers and upper-level field and operations staff members for the franchise, as well as any former Baseball Prospectus staff members who are currently part of the organization.

Position Players

After all that information and a thoughtful bylined essay covering each team, we present our player comments. Each player is listed with the major-league team who employed him as of early January 2019. If a player changed teams after that point via free agency, trade, or any other method, you'll be able to find them in the book for their previous squad.

First, we cover biographical information (age is as of June 30, 2019) before moving onto the stats themselves. Our statistic columns include standard identifying information like **YEAR**, **TEAM**, **LVL** (level of affiliated play) and **AGE** before getting into the numbers. Next, we provide raw, unstranslated numbers like you might find on the back of your dad's baseball cards: **PA** (plate appearances), **R** (runs), **2B** (doubles), **3B** (triples), **HR** (home runs), **RBI** (runs batted in), **BB** (walks), **K** (strikeouts), **SB** (stolen bases) and **CS** (caught stealing). Then we have unadjusted "slash" statistics: **AVG** (batting average), **OBP** (on-base percentage) and **SLG** (slugging percentage).

Just below the stats box is **PECOTA** data, which is discussed further in a following section. After that, it's on to a pithy and always-informative comment written by a member of the Baseball Prospectus staff, before we cover more stats.

The second text box repeats YEAR, TEAM, LVL, AGE, and PA, then moves on to **DRC+** (Deserved Runs Created Plus), which we described earlier as total offensive expected contribution compared to the league average. Next, one of our oldest active metrics, **VORP** (Value Over Replacement Player), considers offensive production, position and plate appearances. In essence, it is the number of runs contributed beyond what a replacement-level player at the same position would contribute if given the same percentage of team plate appearances. VORP does not consider the quality of a player's defense.

BABIP (batting average on balls in play) tells us how often a ball in play fell for a hit, and can help us identify whether a batter may have been lucky or not … but note that high BABIPs also tend to follow the great hitters of our time, as well as speedy singles hitters who put the ball on the ground.

The next item is **BRR** (Baserunning Runs), which covers all of a player's baserunning accomplishments which includes (but isn't limited to) swiped bags and failed attempts. Next is **FRAA** (Fielding Runs Above Average), which also includes the number of games previously played at each position noted in parentheses. Multi-position players have only their two most frequent positions listed here, but their total FRAA number reflects all positions played.

Our last column here is **WARP** (Wins Above Replacement Player). WARP estimates the total value of a player, which means for hitters it takes into account hitting runs above average (calculated using the DRC+ model), BRR and FRAA. Then, it makes an adjustment for positions played and gives the player a credit for plate appearances based upon the difference between "replacement level"¬–which is derived from the quality of players added to a team's roster after the start of the season¬–and the league average.

Catchers

Catchers are a special breed, and thus they have earned their own separate box which displays some of the defensive metrics that we've built just for them. As an example, let's check out J.T. Realmuto.

YEAR	TEAM	P. COUNT	FRM RUNS	BLK RUNS	THRW RUNS	TOT RUNS
2016	MIA	18935	-8.5	1.8	2.1	-5.6
2017	MIA	18959	5.3	1.7	1.0	9.1
2018	MIA	16399	-0.4	0.9	0.1	0.4
2019	PHI	18448	-1.4	1.5	0.7	0.8

The **YEAR** and **TEAM** columns match what you'd find in the other stat box. **P. COUNT** indicates the number of pitches thrown while the catcher was behind the plate, including swinging strikes, fouls, and balls in play. **FRM RUNS** is the total run value the catcher provided (or cost) his team by influencing the umpire to call strikes where other catchers did not. **BLK RUNS** expresses the total run value above or below average for the catcher's ability to prevent wild pitches and passed balls. **THRW RUNS** is calculated using a similar model as the previous two statistics, and it measures a catcher's ability to throw out basestealers but also to dissuade them from testing his arm in the first place. It takes into account factors like the pitcher (including his delivery and pickoff move) and baserunner (who could be as fast as Billy Hamilton or as slow as Yonder Alonso). **TOT RUNS** is the sum of all of the previous three statistics.

Pitchers

Let's give our pitchers a turn, using 2018 NL Cy Young winner Jacob deGrom as our example. Take a look at his first stat block: the first line and the **YEAR**, **TEAM**, **LVL** and **AGE** columns are the same as in the position player example earlier.

Here too, we have a series of columns that display raw, unadjusted statistics compiled by the pitcher over the course of a season: **W** (wins), **L** (losses), **SV** (saves), **G** (games pitched), **GS** (games started), **IP** (innings pitched), **H** (hits allowed) and **HR** (home runs allowed). Next we have two statistics that are rates: **BB/9** (walks per nine innings) and **K/9** (strikeouts per nine innings), before returning to the unadjusted **K** (strikeouts).

Next up is **GB%** (ground ball percentage), which is the percentage of all batted balls that were hit in the ground, including both outs and hits. Remember, this is based on observational data and subject to human error, so please approach this with a healthy dose of skepticism.

BABIP (batting average on balls in play) is calculated using the same methodology as it is for position players, but it often tells us more about a pitcher than it does a hitter. With pitchers, a high BABIP is often due to poor defense or bad luck, and can often be an indicator of potential rebound, and a low BABIP may be cause to expect performance regression. (A typical league-average BABIP is close to .290-.300.)

After a witty 150ish words on the player like only Baseball Prospectus's staff can provide, it's on to that second stat block, which repeats the YEAR, TEAM, LVL, and AGE columns. The metrics **WHIP** (walks plus hits per inning pitched) and **ERA** (earned run average) are old standbys: WHIP measures walks and hits allowed on a per-inning basis, while ERA measures earned runs on a nine-inning basis. Neither of these stats are translated or adjusted.

DRA (Deserved Run Average) was described at length earlier, and measures how many runs the pitcher "deserved" to allow per nine innings. Please note that since we lack all the data points that would make for a "real" DRA for minor-league events, the DRA displayed for minor league partial-seasons is based off of different data. (That data is a modified version of our cFIP metric, which you can find more information about on our website.)

Jacob deGrom   RHP
Born: 06/19/88   Age: 31   Bats: L   Throws: R
Height: 6'4"   Weight: 180   Origin: Round 9, 2010 Draft (#272 overall)

YEAR	TEAM	LVL	AGE	W	L	SV	G	GS	IP	H	HR	BB/9	K/9	K	GB%	BABIP
2016	NYN	MLB	28	7	8	0	24	24	148	142	15	2.2	8.7	143	47%	.312
2017	NYN	MLB	29	15	10	0	31	31	201¹	180	28	2.6	10.7	239	48%	.305
2018	NYN	MLB	30	10	9	0	32	32	217	152	10	1.9	11.2	269	48%	.281
2019	NYN	MLB	31	13	9	0	31	31	186	145	18	2.3	10.7	221	46%	.286

Breakout: 8%   Improve: 29%   Collapse: 28%   Attrition: 6%   MLB: 85%
Comparables: Erik Bedard, A.J. Burnett, CC Sabathia

YEAR	TEAM	LVL	AGE	WHIP	ERA	DRA	WARP	MPH	FB%	WHF	CSP
2016	NYN	MLB	28	1.20	3.04	3.30	3.5	96.3	59.6	12.1	47.2
2017	NYN	MLB	29	1.19	3.53	3.02	5.7	97.2	55.5	14.5	49.5
2018	NYN	MLB	30	0.91	1.70	2.09	8.0	98.2	52.1	16.3	48.4
2019	NYN	MLB	31	1.02	2.91	3.23	3.9	96.6	54.5	14.8	48.2

Just like with hitters, **WARP** (Wins Above Replacement Player) is a total value metric that puts pitchers of all stripes on the same scale as position players. We use DRA as the primary input for our calculation of WARP. You might notice that relief pitchers (due to their limited innings) may have a lower WARP than you were expecting or than you might see in other WARP-like metrics. WARP does not take leverage into account, just the actions a pitcher performs and the expected value of those actions … which ends up judging high-leverage relief pitchers differently than you might imagine given their prestige and market value.

MPH gives you the pitcher's 95th percentile velocity for the noted season, in order to give you an idea of what the *peak* fastball velocity a pitcher possesses. Since this comes from our pitch tracking data, it is not publicly available for minor-league pitchers.

Finally, we display the three new pitching metrics we described earlier. **FB%** (fastball percentage) gives you the percentage of fastballs thrown out of all pitches. **WhiffRt** (whiff rate) tells you the percentage of swinging strikes induced out of all pitches. **CS Prob** (called strike probability) expresses the likelihood of all pitches thrown to result in a called strike, after controlling for factors like handedness, umpire, pitch type, count, and location.

PECOTA

All players have PECOTA projections for 2019, as well as a set of other numbers that describe the performance of comparable players according to PECOTA. All projections for 2019 are for the player at the date we went to press in early January and are projected into the league and park context as indicated by the team abbreviation. All PECOTA projected statistics represent a player's projected major-league performance.

The numbers beneath the player's stats–Breakout, Improve, Collapse, Attrition–are part and parcel of the PECOTA projections. They estimate the likelihood of changes in performance relative to the player's previously-established level of production, based on the performance of comparable players:

Breakout Rate is the percent change that a player's production will improve by at least 20 percent relative to the weighted average of his performance over his most recent seasons.

Improve Rate is the percent chance that a player's production will improve at all relative to his baseline performance. A player who is expected to perform just the same as he has in the recent past will have an Improve Rate of 50 percent.

Collapse Rate is the percent chance that a position player's production will decline by at least 25 percent relative to his baseline performance.

Attrition Rate operates on playing time rather than performance. Specifically, it measures the likelihood that a player's playing time will decrease by at least 50 percent relative to his established level.

Breakout Rate and Collapse Rate can sometimes be counterintuitive for players who have already experienced a radical change in performance level. It's also worth noting that the projected decline in a player's rate performances might not be indicative of an expected decline in underlying ability or skill, but could just be an anticipated correction following a breakout season.

MLB% is the percentage of similar players who played in the major leagues in their relevant season.

The final pieces of information are the player's three highest-scoring comparable players as determined by PECOTA. All comparables represent a snapshot of how the listed player was performing at the same age as the current player, so if a 23-year-old pitcher is compared to Bartolo Colon, he's actually being compared to a 23-year-old Colon, not the version that pitched for the Rangers in 2018, nor to Colon's career as a whole.

A few points about pitcher projections. First, we aren't yet projecting peak velocity, so that column will be blank in the PECOTA lines. Second, projecting DRA is trickier than evaluating past performance, because it is unclear how deserving each pitcher will be of his anticipated outcomes. However, we know that another DRA-related statistic–contextual FIP or cFIP–estimates future run scoring very well. So for PECOTA, the projected DRA figures you see are based on the past cFIPs generated by the pitcher and comparable players over time, along with the other factors described above.

Lineouts

In each chapter's Lineouts section, you'll find abbreviated text comments, as well as most of same information you'd find in our full player comments. We limit the stats boxes in this section to only including the 2018 information for each player.

Exclusive Player Visualizations

In our constant battle to provide you with new and interesting baseball content you can't find anywhere else, we've added a trio of data visualizations to each hitter's entry in these books and a pair of visualizations for each pitcher.

For hitters, you'll find three new infographics. The first is each player's **Batted Ball Distribution**, which displays the five major sections of the field: LF (left), LCF (left center), CF (center), RCF (right center), and RF (right). The percentage indicated tells us what percentage of batted balls from that hitter fell within that part of the field during the 2018 season. We've also included the hitter's slugging percentage on balls in play (also called **SLGCON**) for that part of the field.

You'll also see two heatmaps: **Strike Zone vs LHP** and **Strike Zone vs RHP**. These heat maps represent a view of the strike zone from behind the catcher. Areas where there is a darker coloration represent the places where a higher percentage of pitches resulted in hits. In other words, the heatmap represents a hitter's "sweet spots" for getting hits against either left-handed or right-handed pitchers, depending on the image.

Pitchers get two images that help explain what their pitches look like from a hitter's perspective: **Pitch Shape vs LHH** and **Pitch Shape vs RHH**. These images show you the shape and the "tunneling" effect of each pitcher's offerings from the batter's perspective. For each type of pitch that a pitcher throws (represented by an indicator shape), there's a set of dots indicating the flight path, where each dot represents a 0.01-second interval. This maps the average trajectory and speed of an offering, ending where the ball crosses the plate. The solid black box represents the regular strike zone, while the gray contour lines indicate the range of locations that a pitcher typically works in.

Below the image, we provide a bit more detailed information about each pitcher's average offering in the **Pitch Types** box. Here, we also list each of the pitcher's major offerings under the **Type** column.

- **Fastballs** (which usually refers to the four-seam variation)
- **Sinkers** and/or two-seam fastballs
- **Cutters** (which could include "hard" cutters like cut fastballs and "soft" cutters that resemble hard sliders)
- **Changeups** (not including most splitters)
- **Splitters** (split-fingered pitches, forkballs, and some split-changes)
- **Sliders** and/or slurves
- **Curveballs** (including spike-curveballs and knuckle-curveballs, as well as some slurvy curves)
- **Slow curveballs** and/or eephus pitches
- **Knuckleballs**
- **Screwballs**

The **Freq** column indicates the percentage of overall pitches that fall into each of those type categories; if a pitcher has a 16.55% score for changeups, then that's the percent of all pitches that he throws as changeups. **Velo** is exactly what you think it is: the average miles per hour for each pitch type. **H Mov** is the number of inches of horizontal movement on the average pitch of that type, while **V Mov** is the number of inches of vertical movement on the average pitch of that type. (At Baseball Prospectus, we measure this over the long flight of the ball and include gravity into the V Mov number in order to give you the most realistic representation of what the pitch *actually* does.)

If you're wondering about the second number in brackets, that's the index for that velocity or movement compared to the league average. Like DRC+, a score of 100 means that the speed or movement is about the same as league average, while a higher score means that there's higher velocity or movement than the league average. Numbers below 100 indicate less velocity or movement than the league average.

Part 1: Team Analysis

Rand McNally Reader

Table for Three: Previewing the 2019 Milwaukee Brewers

J.P. Breen, Paul Noonan and Sean Roberts

SEAN ROBERTS: I guess we should start with the big elephant in the room, the signing that took everyone by surprise this winter. Will Alex Claudio be enough to reinforce the bullpen?

Kidding aside, the Yasmani Grandal contract has so far given GM David Stearns his second title in a row of "best signing of the winter," after adding Cain last year. And while PECOTA likes Grandal to the tune of a 4-win improvement over last year's catching production, I'm left wondering a bit if that's enough to offset the pretty generous regression projected from Aguilar, Yelich, Cain, and whatever is going on at second base.

J.P. BREEN: The catching position offered the best opportunity for improvement on the roster. Needless to say, adding Grandal transforms the position to one of strength, and the fact that they were able to do so without shipping top prospects (looking at you, Philly) only adds to the benefit. I remain worried about Grandal's penchant for the passed ball. Catching defense isn't synonymous with pitch framing, so it will be interesting to see whether Brewers' pitchers are willing to spike breaking balls in high-leverage spots. But, yeah, I have no qualms labeling the Grandal signing the best of the winter, even if it simultaneously depresses me due to what it means for the broader baseball economy.

With that said, are we buying what PECOTA is selling at second base? It's pessimistic at the very least.

PAUL NOONAN: The Brewers were so creative with second last year, and with Mike Moustakas now officially back in the fold, they will be again. Fortunately when it comes to creativity, they are unmatched. Moustakas has already taken some reps there, and we know Shaw can play there in a pinch. I expect a lot of Shaw/Moose early with Hernan Perez stepping in late to solidify the defense, at least until Keston Hiura is ready to go.

While PECOTA is a down on Hiura, it's down on him in a really weird way. I think the comp to Jonathan Schoop is instructive as to the limits of such projections, because in the long run it's almost a sure thing that Hiura makes more contact than Schoop. What PECOTA sees isn't likely to last with Hiura's hit tool, and I like him to be better than the projection once he arrives. If he's not, they now have a decent plan B in place.

My biggest worry offensively is actually over at first base, where Aguilar seems unlikely to repeat. That and Braun.

SEAN: Braun is actually a fascinating case for me this year. It's probably not fair to him or Statcast, but I do tend to think of this in my own head as a test case for what these data "mean" for hitters like Braun. Last year his exit velocity and hard-hit rate were both in the top 7% of the league, while his expected batting average and expected slugging percentage were statcast-era highs. For whatever reason, it just never really showed up in the results, as he posted career lows in batting average and on-base percentage, and had his second-lowest year slugging.

Based on the underlying on-field data I'm intrigued enough to think he could be good to be somewhere between his 108 DRC+ from last year and his 125 and 129 he put up in 2015 and 2016, respectively. It's weird to think of a 35-year old as a breakout candidate, but it's not hard to imagine him putting the skillset together with a tweaked swing to break out as a "new" older Ryan Braun, if that makes sense. Are there other players you all are looking at as potential breakouts or significant changes in performance this year?

J.P.: Back to Braun for a quick moment. He is an odd case because he's both injury prone and aging, which understandably has caused people to accept his downturn in performance without interrogating it. The Statcast numbers had Braun with the eighth-highest negative gap between his wOBA and expected wOBA, and his .274 BABIP was over 50 points worse than his career average (and almost 20 points lower than it had ever been as a professional). Moreover, any Brewers fan who watched games in 2018 saw Braun hit rockets right at outfield defenders across the diamond. That frustration motivated Braun to join the #LaunchAngleRevolution this winter. Whether changing his launch angle results in anything meaningful is a giant shrug emoji, but it highlights the seeming disconnect between the on-field performance and the numerous analytics that are publicly available.

In terms of other breakout candidates, I'm ready for Milwaukee to let Brandon Woodruff loose in the rotation. He allowed one run in September and struck out 20 batters in 12.1 postseason innings. *Brooks Baseball* clocked his average fastball at 96 mph in 2018, and his slider picked up 2-3 miles per hour from where it was in August 2017. The right-hander even had a 3.16 DRA. PECOTA projects Woodruff to post a 3.51 ERA, which PECOTA sees being the best of the Brewers' starters. I think that's a bit rosy, considering most of his 2018 work came out of the bullpen. Woodruff also still struggles against lefties due to a lack of a consistent third pitch. But he's someone who I think can lock down a mid-rotation spot this year.

SEAN: Woodruff's PECOTA projection really did stand out. He's also projected for the highest WARP among all Brewer pitchers for next year at 1.8. It's really surprising to me that a lot of the chatter around the rotation kind of has him as a 5th starter or swingman type that's in and out of the bullpen. Of course, roles are essentially meaningless on Craig Counsell's staff, but because of the September he had (and really, second half with an elite ground ball rate while striking out better than a batter per inning after his early ups and downs), I thought he'd be in the team's number 3 or 4 spot going into spring, at least. Either way the pitching staff remains the biggest question mark for the season and I'm not quite sure how to account for their depth or what the roles will be moving forward.

PAUL: Obviously PECOTA is seeing Woodruff's bat speed and contact skills. Kidding aside, I think the proper way to look at the Brewer starting staff is to work backwards a bit. Many (myself included) probably oversold their reliance on the pen last season as the wave of the future, but while they are a pen-first team, starters are still important. While a team like the Cubs has relievers working in service to the starters, the Brewer starters work to serve the bullpen, and not having enough starter innings hurts the pen. I think a guy like Woodruff, who does need work on a third pitch as JP mentoned, really benefit by being in this particular system. He'll probably blow teams away for 4.66 innings per game, which gives some support to that PECOTA projection, but I think it's important to note that this team would benefit from another starter or two who could reliably give the pen a break. Chacin is that, to an extent, but it's easy to forget that Mike Zagurski actually pitched a few meaningful innings out of the pen last season, and limiting such things in the future would be helpful.

One thing to be excited about PECOTA-wise is Corey Knebel. Josh Hader is projected to have the third best DRA this season, but Knebel is right there with him at sixth overall (projected 2.99). Having two super-dominant arms in that pen probably benefits the Brewers more than just about any other team, and my biggest worry, if the starters are Chacin plus young guys, is simply that they are forced to go to this well too often. In any case, I'm with JP on Woodruff, though I'm also a big Corbin Burnes fan, even if PECOTA really isn't, which strikes me as odd. DRA is especially cynical (projected 4.69), but he throws hard and gets a ton of ground balls into the Brewer shift. I do worry that another year of grinding the pen takes its toll, and would like to see another starter. Do you both think they have enough to work with rotation-wise?

SEAN: Each member of the staff has such a huge variance of outcomes and that feels right to me. For instance, PECOTA has Jimmy Nelson's 10th percentile outcome as a 5.13 DRA, and his 90th percentile is 2.95. Neither would shock me, as there are so many unknowns with him coming back from his injury. But that's really the story of most of the rotation's pitchers, whether coming back from injury or not.

I think the Brewers are banking on quantity of pitchers with big error bars on either side and expecting some of the veterans like Chase Anderson to have bounce backs in line with their career averages -or- young guys like Freddy Peralta to take a step forward (and how about his 50th percentile projection of 3.59 DRA!).

All that is to say I think it's a harder-than-average to predict rotation. However, they simply have so many options (Supak, Burnes, Guerra) to back up the top seven that it's reasonable to think they could lean heavily on the bullpen and get away with it again while still acknowledging the certainty of a top-line starter could at least give them more predictability and role flexibility.

J.P.: Paul makes a smart observation with Corbin Burnes. While the right-hander did have a .232 BABIP in 2018, it's worth noting that DRA liked his performance quite a bit (3.39 DRA). Beyond that, Burnes has many of the core attributes for which you'd look when hunting for a potential breakout pitcher. His fastball sits in the mid-90s; he has a hard, sharp slider; his swinging-strike rate was 15.2 percent last year; he generates ground balls; and he had a 7.2-percent walk rate. Beyond his big-league performance, Burnes has even shown a potentially average third pitch. So, yeah, he has all the makings of a mid-rotation starter—maybe a bit more if you really squint and dream a bit—in the coming years.

Much of our conversation has been positive, which is understandable given the team's surprising NL Central crown last season. But where are things potentially going to go wrong?

PAUL: This is a tricky one just because I don't really think they were lucky last season, and so there isn't a huge regression candidate out there, at least not an obvious one. If Aguilar fell off, it wouldn't be surprising, but it also wouldn't be fatal to the season. They had so many black holes at the back of the order with Kratz/Arcia that it's difficult to see how the offense overall could really disappoint. I think my biggest worry is counterintuitively probably the relievers. The bullpen has added importance for the Brewers, and while it's undeniably a strength, if Josh Hader were to go down, it would look a lot different. Having your team's key strength rest on a fundamentally variable aspect of baseball is always going to be a bit risky. Does anyone have bigger offensive concerns than I do?

SEAN: I agree with you on the bullpen, but would expand my concern to include Jeffress and Knebel as well. If any one of those "big three" run into problems (and let's not forget that Knebel was sent down to AAA as recently as last year), this is a different team.

As far as the offense, I look at the regression PECOTA has built in with Yelich, Aguilar, and Shaw all taking steps back, and Braun and Arcia taking slight steps forward in WARP of less than a win each, and you can make the case that's a problem. Then you come back to the 4-WARP projected upgrade at catcher and that's hard to overestimate the impact that would have on the offense. So, given the potential for bullpen volatility and some offensive uncertainty, where do we see the Brewers ending up this year?

I think the rotation and "out-getting" roles are serviceable, with the depth and young pitchers that will be ready to contribute over a full season and a few positive surprises sprinkled in. However, the back end of the bullpen is more volatile and the division itself is much tougher with the Reds and Cardinals taking significant steps forward. I'll say 86-76 and just barely misses the second wild card.

PAUL: One thing we didn't touch on was their outstanding managing. Counsell is likely the best manager in baseball, and while the Brewers may have some built-in volatility, they have the best possible person in place to manage it properly. They've shown limited tolerance for failed experiments and struggling players, but they're also not afraid to bring them right back into the fold when they're right, as with Knebel last season. For that reason, I like the upside, and I think they win a very competitive division at 89-73.

J.P.: Counsell has been one of the best managers in Major League Baseball. He communicates well, fosters a positive clubhouse environment, and bridges the information gap between the analytics guys and the on-the-field guys exceedingly well. Prior to the Moustakas signing, I saw the Brewers as an 85- or 86-win team with a high margin for error on either side due to the question marks in the pitching staff. Moose adds more redundancy to the lineup. He ensures that the team has answers if Jesus Aguilar takes a step backward, or if Keston Hiura scuffles upon his big-league debut, or if Travis Shaw becomes strictly a platoon player. I think he raises the floor a bit and should improve the overall offense until Hiura gets the call. I'll say the Brewers finish 87-75 and finish second behind the St. Louis Cardinals in a wide-open division.

Performance Graphs

2018 Hit List Ranking

Committed Payroll (in millions)

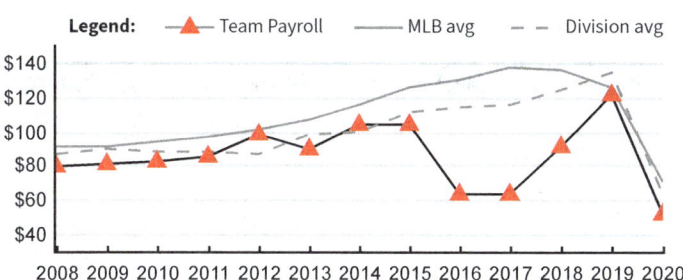

Farm System Ranking

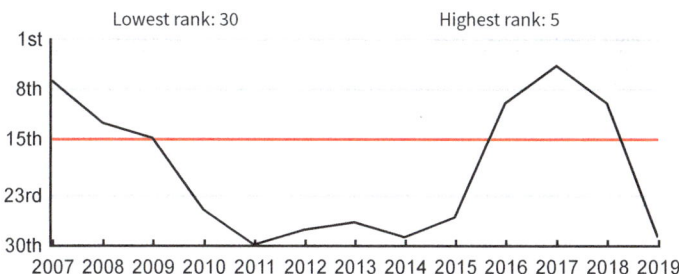

2018 Team Performance

ACTUAL STANDINGS

Team	W	L	Pct
MIL	96	67	.588
CHN	95	68	.582
SLN	88	74	.543
PIT	82	79	.509
CIN	67	95	.413

THIRD-ORDER STANDINGS

Team	W	L	Pct
MIL	93	70	.570
CHN	92	71	.564
SLN	83	79	.512
PIT	78	83	.484
CIN	71	91	.438

TOP HITTERS

Player	WARP
Christian Yelich	4.8
Lorenzo Cain	4.5
Jesus Aguilar	3.6

TOP PITCHERS

Player	WARP
Josh Hader	2.7
Jeremy Jeffress	2
Jhoulys Chacin	1.8

VITAL STATISTICS

Statistic Name	Value	Rank
Pythagenpat	.562	9th
Runs Scored per Game	4.63	12th
Runs Allowed per Game	4.04	8th
Deserved Runs Created Plus	98	11th
Deserved Run Average	4.26	12th
Fielding Independent Pitching	3.96	13th
Defensive Efficiency Rating	.721	4th
Batter Age	28.9	24th
Pitcher Age	28.7	17th
Salary	$91.0M	26th
Marginal $ per Marginal Win	$1.6M	28th
Disabled List Days	$1,025.0M	13th
$ on DL	16%	15th

2019 Team Projections

PROJECTED STANDINGS

Team	W	L	Pct	+/-
MIL	**88**	**74**	**.543**	**-8**
SLN	85	77	.524	-3
CIN	81	81	.500	+14
PIT	80	82	.493	-2
CHN	79	83	.487	-16

TOP PROJECTED HITTERS

Player	WARP
Lorenzo Cain	4.7
Yasmani Grandal	4.2
Christian Yelich	4.1

TOP PROJECTED PITCHERS

Player	WARP
Josh Hader	2.0
Brandon Woodruff	1.7
Corey Knebel	1.3

FARM SYSTEM REPORT

Top Prospect	Number of Top 101 Prospects
Keston Hiura, #6	1

KEY DEDUCTIONS

Player	WARP
Jonathan Schoop	2.0
Curtis Granderson	1.3
Domingo Santana	0.8
Wade Miley	0.6
Joakim Soria	0.6
Jordan Lyles	0.4

KEY ADDITIONS

Player	WARP
Yasmani Grandal	4.2
Ben Gamel	0.4
Alex Claudio	0.3

Team Personnel

General Manager
David Stearns

VP, Assistant General Manager
Matt Arnold

Senior Advisor
Doug Melvin

Manager
Craig Counsell

BP Alumni
James Fisher
Adam Hayes
Greg Goldstein
Mike Groopman
Shawn Hoffman
Matt Kleine
Will Siskel
Dan Turkenkopf

Miller Park Stats

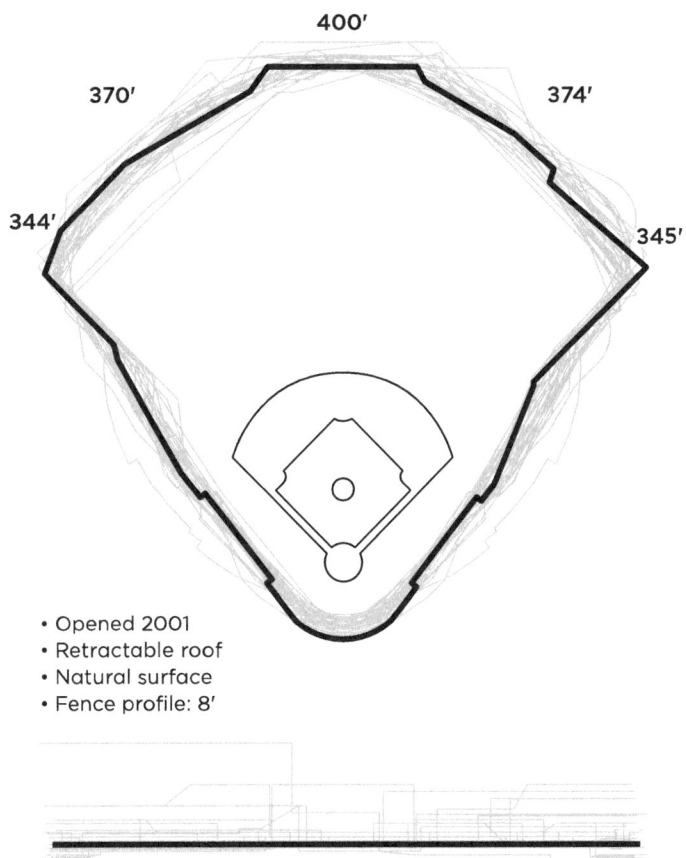

- Opened 2001
- Retractable roof
- Natural surface
- Fence profile: 8'

Three-Year Park Factors

Runs	Runs/RH	Runs/LH	HR/RH	HR/LH
102	102	100	102	112

Brewers Team Analysis

You've all read *Moneyball*, right? If you haven't, it's probably two shelves down from the shelf that you picked this book off. It's the story from back in the heyday of the Backstreet Boys about a team in a small market that managed to punch above its weight by finding value in places that no one else thought to look. At the time, the A's exploited the fact that everyone in baseball was too in love with batting average, when OBP was a much better stat. As (gasp!) both *Moneyball* and "I Want It That Way" are reaching the age where they would be legal to vote, it seems trite to talk about the problems of batting average, especially among the people who would be picking up a copy of *Baseball Prospectus*, but sometimes all you need is one decent idea.

The 2018 Milwaukee Brewers played in the smallest of all the 30 MLB media markets and yet somehow won the NL Central division and came within one game of the World Series and did it with one of the lowest payrolls in the game. And they seemed to do it on the back of one fairly simple idea. They found players that—for some strange reason—other teams didn't want. It's not that no one had ever figured this one out before. Baseball is filled with stories the ones who got away, and the Brewers seemed to have a knack for finding "perfectly respectable" players from the discard pile, to the point where it was almost seen as a weakness. If you have too many perfectly respectable players around, then the marginal upgrade that comes from a really good player isn't quite as large, and so finding a match between the marginal gain and the salary that the player commands on the open market becomes harder. Somehow though, the Brewers struck gold in the bargain pile.

When the Marlins inexplicably decided to trade their entire outfield, the Brewers staged the *coup* of the off-season. They ended up with Christian Yelich who was signed for several years at an entirely reasonable price, even if one believed that he was a good-but-not-great outfielder, which is what WARP suggested he had been to that point. Sure, he cost the team four prospects, but Yelich responded by nearly winning the Triple Crown. (And since this is *Baseball Prospectus*, let's throw in the obligatory note that he also led the National League in slugging percentage, OPS, WARP among position players, and came in third in OBP.)

There's even a case to be made that Yelich was even more valuable to the Brewers than his WARP would have suggested. Yelich played mostly in the corner outfield spots in 2018, and was compared to other corner outfielders when it came time to define "replacement level" for his performance. What WARP wasn't able to see was that in 2017, he was the Marlins' primary center fielder and acquitted himself decently well at the position. In 2018, he didn't need to play much center, as the Brewers also employed Lorenzo Cain, but he *could have* if the Brewers had needed him to. That extra glove in his locker, even though he rarely used it, meant that the Brewers could feel comfortable carrying Domingo Santana—a corner guy—as their fourth outfielder. Santana turned in a league-average performance with the bat, which is a nice thing to have coming off the bench. But for a moment, assume that Yelich had gotten hurt early in the year. The Brewers probably would have slid Santana into the starting lineup on a regular basis, but they would have had to replace Yelich on the roster with someone who could "handle center" because they didn't have their *de facto* backup center fielder any more. That probably would have meant more time on the roster for someone like Keon Broxton. So if Yelich would have practically had to be replaced by a center fielder on the roster and because he effectively allowed the Brewers to roster the better hitting Santana rather than Broxton, shouldn't his replacement level be the somewhat more forgiving center field one?

If Yelich wasn't enough, lightning struck twice in the Brewers outfield, when Lorenzo Cain landed (back) at Miller Park for a contract that was surprisingly affordable, given Cain's track record. Cain was widely known as an excellent defender in center, a good baserunner, and to have an above-average OBP, which is the sort of combination that a 5-win season is made of, but the "usual suspects" in free agency didn't really have an opening in center field and the 2017-2018 off-season was a winter of tan—we're not supposed to use the "T" word—rebuilding for a lot of teams. A lot of clubs were sitting on the sidelines. In a world where Sabermetric teams are always supposed to live for the future and hoard their dollars and prospects so that in three years they can hoard the same dollars and a new set of prospects, the Brewers realized that they had an opening. It's not like 5-win players grow on trees, and yet few teams seemed to want the one that was sitting right there in front of them. When everyone else is waiting, there is value in action.

But then if you look up and down the rest of the Brewers lineup from 2018, you see several other guys who were claimed and reclaimed from other teams, not because they were bad, but because the other team didn't have room. Jesus Aguilar hit 30 home runs for the Indians AAA team in 2016, but was stuck behind Carlos Santana and Edwin Encarnacion. The raw power was obviously there and there was enough OBP in the bat to make it work. At age 28, he blossomed. Travis Shaw had a perfectly respectable year for the Red Sox in 2016 when he was asked to fill-in for mega-signing Pablo Sandoval, but when Sandoval and his contract came back in 2017, Shaw was suddenly available and was gotten for Tyler Thornburg. Prototypical journeyman backup catcher Erik Kratz—the

Brewers represented his 8th team in 9 years—logged the most plate appearances of his career at age-38 after someone realized that he was still one of the best pitch framers in baseball.

All you need is one good idea.

On the pitching side, the Brewers' big idea was that there were pitchers out in the universe who were under-valued because they were throwing the wrong pitches. Jhoulys Chacin, who had been the rare "pitcher who had a couple good years in Colorado" turned from castoff into the team's ace by doubling the usage of his slider, which the numbers showed had always been his best pitch. Jeremy Jeffress, back for his third tour of duty with the Brewers having been twice traded away previously, stopped relying primarily on his fastball and started throwing his curveball more. Junior Guerra came to the Brewers in 2016 and became less of a stinker by throwing a sinker. Wade Miley started throwing a cutter nearly half the time. Coupled with the emergence of Josh Hader in a throwback "let him throw two innings" relief role, the Brewers sewed together a silken pitching staff—and a decent one, they gave up the 8th fewest runs in baseball—out of what appeared to be a collection of sow's ears.

The Brewers aren't the only ones doing this. The ever-popular #NewMoneyball has moved from identifying players who are already doing something that people aren't valuing properly to identifying players who are not doing something (or doing it enough) but could and are being valued for what they have done rather than what they might become. The much-discussed "Launch Angle Revolution" was little more than hitting coaches talking to a few players and saying "Hey, why don't you try hitting a few more fly balls. Some of them will leave the park" but it turned several floundering careers around. This is the pitching equivalent, though it's gotten less attention.

What the Brewers are doing is riding the shockwave caused by the collision of a couple of trends. Fastball usage has declined by nearly 10 percentage points between 2002 and 2018. It's not that pitchers have stopped throwing fastballs altogether, but now the ol' number 1 accounts for just a little more than half of the pitches thrown. Strangely though, the percentage of balls put into play that started their lives as fastballs has gone up. While most players will say that they "sit fastball" this is evidence that the fastball chair has gotten a lot more comfy for hitters. If hitters really are sitting fastball, why give them one? And if you have a pitcher who has an ineffective fastball and a better off-speed pitch of some sort, why not have him throw the pitch that is both better and not what the hitter is hoping for?

The fascinating piece about the Brewers' success story in 2018 wasn't that it heralded some new sort of thinking in baseball. The Brewers identified a couple of player types that were under-appreciated and loaded up on them. They found a couple of important trends and exploited them. They picked up little bits of extra value that even the "advanced" metrics didn't see. Add a little luck (no one gets by without a little bit of luck in baseball) and suddenly a team that was largely unfancied is knocking on the door of the World Series. In a world where Moneyball had never been written, but where some enterprising author wanted to write a book with the same message, they could have replaced the millennial A's with the 2018 Brew Crew.

—*Russell Carleton is an author of Baseball Prospectus.*

Part 2: Player Analysis

Milwaukee Brewers 2019

Jesus Aguilar 1B

Born: 06/30/90   Age: 29   Bats: R   Throws: R
Height: 6'3"   Weight: 250   Origin: International Free Agent, 2007

YEAR	TEAM	LVL	AGE	PA	R	2B	3B	HR	RBI	BB	K	SB	CS	AVG/OBP/SLG
2016	COH	AAA	26	578	62	26	0	30	92	53	110	0	0	.247/.319/.472
2016	CLE	MLB	26	6	0	0	0	0	0	0	1	0	0	.000/.000/.000
2017	MIL	MLB	27	311	40	15	2	16	52	25	94	0	0	.265/.331/.505
2018	MIL	MLB	28	566	80	25	0	35	108	58	143	0	0	.274/.352/.539
2019	MIL	MLB	29	560	68	24	2	26	80	51	145	0	0	.242/.318/.455

Breakout: 10%   Improve: 25%   Collapse: 18%   Attrition: 21%   MLB: 54%
Comparables: Darin Ruf, Jake Fox, Brandon Moss

The best part about Aguilar is that he shouldn't be here. Of course, with logical scouting grades and assessments of potential career prototypes, the bulk of the comments in this here *Annual* could highlight shortcomings, reasons things shouldn't work. Aguilar is a great test of your threshold for this type of thinking; first as a surefire designated hitter who couldn't possibly find value on a National League bench that demands flexibility; then, as an everyday first baseman who stole a job and couldn't possibly be more than a one-year wonder (as evidenced by a brutal second-half in 2017); and now, as an All-Star who even mitigated the second-half collapse narrative with an excellent August and solid September in 2018.

YEAR	TEAM	LVL	AGE	PA	DRC+	VORP	BABIP	BRR	FRAA	WARP
2016	COH	AAA	26	578	114	7.8	.255	-3.0	1B(120): -1.0, 3B(2): 0.3	0.4
2016	CLE	MLB	26	6	85	-1.7	.000	0.0	1B(7): -0.3	0.0
2017	MIL	MLB	27	311	101	12.8	.337	0.4	1B(77): 1.2, 3B(1): 0.0	0.7
2018	MIL	MLB	28	566	135	35.0	.309	-1.1	1B(132): 3.6, 3B(5): 0.0	3.6
2019	MIL	MLB	29	560	106	15.4	.285	-1.0	1B 0	1.5

Jesus Aguilar, continued

Batted Ball Distribution

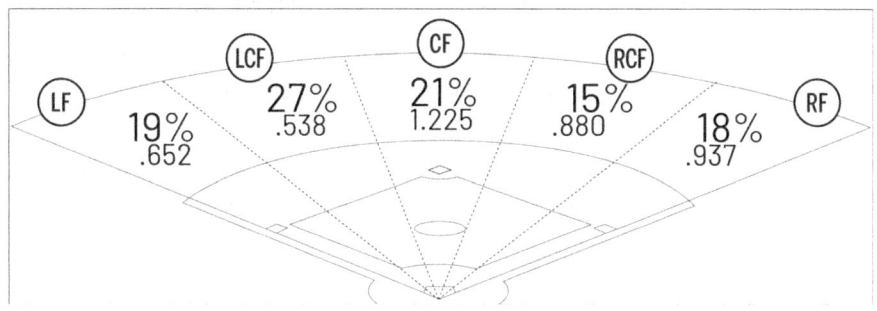

Strike Zone vs LHP **Strike Zone vs RHP**

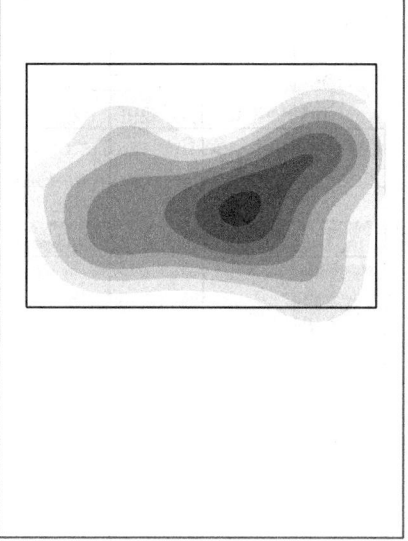

Orlando Arcia SS

Born: 08/04/94   Age: 24   Bats: R   Throws: R
Height: 6'0"   Weight: 165   Origin: International Free Agent, 2010

YEAR	TEAM	LVL	AGE	PA	R	2B	3B	HR	RBI	BB	K	SB	CS	AVG/OBP/SLG
2016	CSP	AAA	21	440	59	19	6	8	53	29	77	15	8	.267/.320/.403
2016	MIL	MLB	21	216	21	10	3	4	17	15	47	8	0	.219/.273/.358
2017	MIL	MLB	22	548	56	17	2	15	53	36	100	14	7	.277/.324/.407
2018	CSP	AAA	23	96	16	5	1	2	8	10	15	2	1	.341/.417/.494
2018	MIL	MLB	23	366	32	16	0	3	30	15	87	7	4	.236/.268/.307
2019	MIL	MLB	24	439	49	16	2	10	43	31	93	10	4	.241/.299/.366

Breakout: 11%   Improve: 62%   Collapse: 3%   Attrition: 6%   MLB: 98%
Comparables: Ketel Marte, Asdrubal Cabrera, Everth Cabrera

Arcia could push the envelope as a throwback, defense-only shortstop even during an era that values defensive metrics. The glove was his only strength for the bulk of 2018, so much so that Arcia earned two demotions to Triple-A to figure out the bat. Judging Arcia by FRAA, he ranked in the 90th percentile of shortstops during each of his age-21 through age-23 seasons. Rare company shares this feat: Here lie legacy shortstops like Cal Ripken Jr. (1982-1984), current superstar Francisco Lindor, plus Roy McMillan (1951-1953), Milt Bolling (1952-1954) and Tim Foli (1972-1974). Should Arcia continue to bat according to his second-half slash of .290/.320/.386 he may have a chance to follow this category of defense-first shortstop comparison, transporting him to an era that challenges contemporary player valuations.

YEAR	TEAM	LVL	AGE	PA	DRC+	VORP	BABIP	BRR	FRAA	WARP
2016	CSP	AAA	21	440	82	12.2	.312	-0.5	SS(92): 6.8, 2B(7): 0.7	1.0
2016	MIL	MLB	21	216	66	-1.6	.267	-1.0	SS(53): 3.8	0.3
2017	MIL	MLB	22	548	94	26.8	.317	2.1	SS(152): 6.8	3.0
2018	CSP	AAA	23	96	130	10.8	.397	2.3	SS(22): 3.9	1.3
2018	MIL	MLB	23	366	59	-0.3	.305	2.0	SS(116): 3.8	0.4
2019	MIL	MLB	24	439	80	7.5	.288	0.2	SS 6	1.2

Orlando Arcia, continued

Batted Ball Distribution

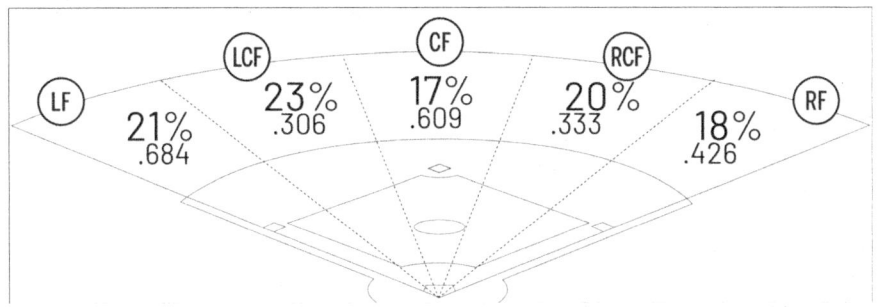

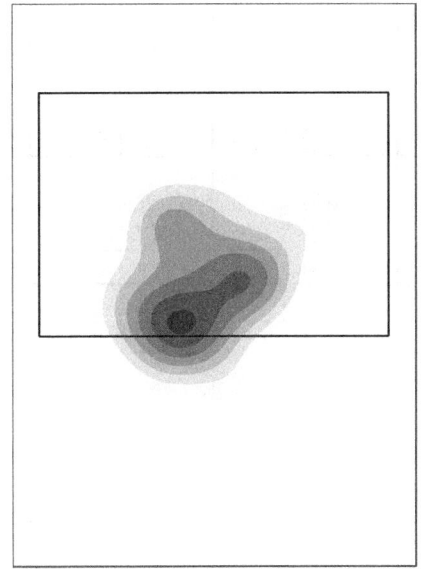

Strike Zone vs LHP

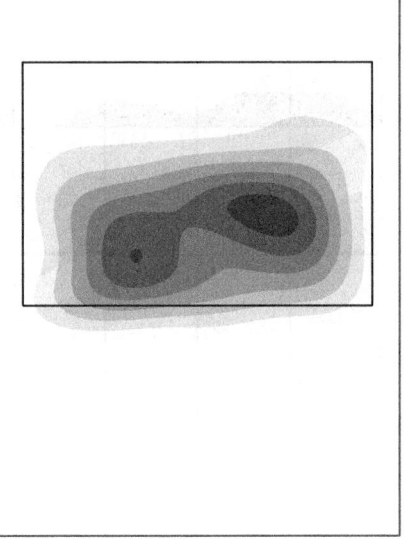

Strike Zone vs RHP

Ryan Braun LF

Born: 11/17/83 Age: 35 Bats: R Throws: R
Height: 6'2" Weight: 205 Origin: Round 1, 2005 Draft (#5 overall)

YEAR	TEAM	LVL	AGE	PA	R	2B	3B	HR	RBI	BB	K	SB	CS	AVG/OBP/SLG
2016	MIL	MLB	32	564	80	23	3	30	91	46	98	16	5	.305/.365/.538
2017	MIL	MLB	33	425	58	28	2	17	52	38	76	12	4	.268/.336/.487
2018	MIL	MLB	34	447	59	25	1	20	64	34	85	11	5	.254/.313/.469
2019	MIL	MLB	35	464	59	21	2	16	57	41	91	14	5	.259/.329/.434

Breakout: 0% Improve: 25% Collapse: 18% Attrition: 20% MLB: 90%
Comparables: Steve Pearce, Dusty Baker, Monte Irvin

Thanks to a reported late-season mechanical adjustment which launched Braun into the fly-ball revolution, this wily veteran will receive one more player comment praising power and overall batting ability. Maybe he's born with it. In August, the superstar-turned-upstart leader began compiling the hits once more. The power placed an exclamation point on Milwaukee's improbable National League Central surge, and when it was all said and done those final two months read .283/.362/.538. The aging curve seemed to bend Braun out of his comfort zone, but don't count out the silver slugger if those swing mechanics stick.

YEAR	TEAM	LVL	AGE	PA	DRC+	VORP	BABIP	BRR	FRAA	WARP
2016	MIL	MLB	32	564	129	45.7	.326	1.4	LF(127): -3.7, RF(2): -0.1	3.1
2017	MIL	MLB	33	425	104	20.1	.292	0.5	LF(95): -3.7	1.0
2018	MIL	MLB	34	447	108	17.5	.274	-0.8	LF(93): -4.9, 1B(18): -0.4	0.8
2019	MIL	MLB	35	464	108	19.2	.295	0.8	LF -3	1.7

Ryan Braun, continued

Batted Ball Distribution

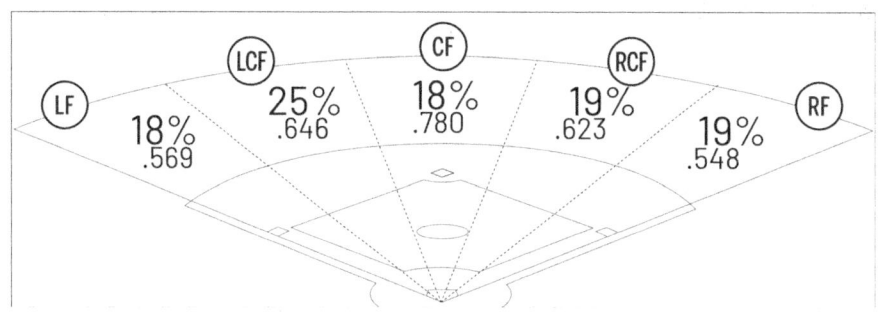

Strike Zone vs LHP

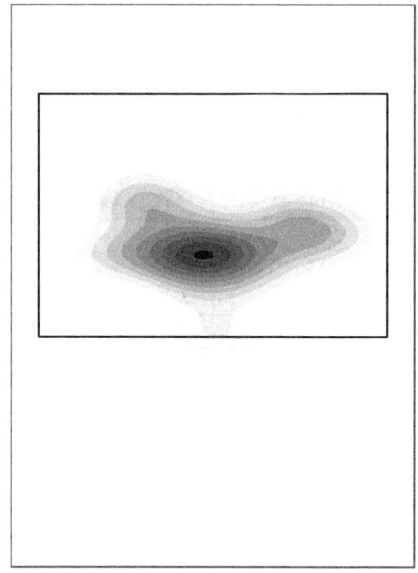

Strike Zone vs RHP

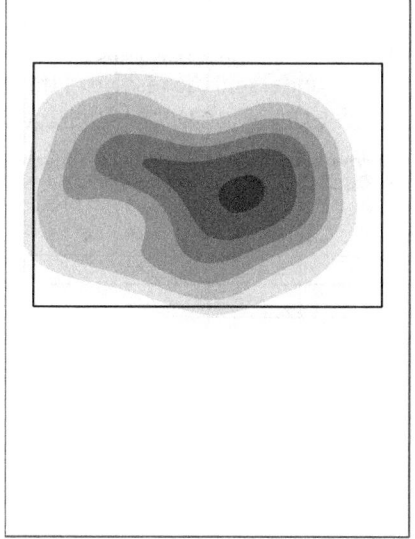

Lorenzo Cain CF

Born: 04/13/86 Age: 33 Bats: R Throws: R
Height: 6'2" Weight: 205 Origin: Round 17, 2004 Draft (#496 overall)

YEAR	TEAM	LVL	AGE	PA	R	2B	3B	HR	RBI	BB	K	SB	CS	AVG/OBP/SLG
2016	KCA	MLB	30	434	56	19	1	9	56	31	84	14	5	.287/.339/.408
2017	KCA	MLB	31	645	86	27	5	15	49	54	100	26	2	.300/.363/.440
2018	MIL	MLB	32	620	90	25	2	10	38	71	94	30	7	.308/.395/.417
2019	MIL	MLB	33	634	87	27	3	13	59	63	113	25	5	.278/.355/.406

Breakout: 0% Improve: 27% Collapse: 24% Attrition: 16% MLB: 94%
Comparables: Earle Combs, Johnny Damon, Chuck Hinton

When Cain broke out with the 2015 Royals, the elite center fielder served as Kansas City's third batter. Cain grew into a trusty veteran while serving in that run-production role, ultimately batting .299 with a 7.2 percent walk rate from 2015-2017. When the Brewers signed Cain to a reasonable $80 million deal during the ice cold offseason, they asked if Cain could serve as an on-base guy; Cain naturally responded with an 11.5 percent walk rate and .395 OBP. The veteran sacrificed some power for that discipline, but that's just splitting hairs as Cain produced arguably the best offensive season of his career during a low-key MVP campaign. Critics of Cain's contract point out that speed ages poorly, but they undersold the resolve of this shape-shifter; now Cain's elite plate discipline can help ease the other lumps on the aging curve.

YEAR	TEAM	LVL	AGE	PA	DRC+	VORP	BABIP	BRR	FRAA	WARP
2016	KCA	MLB	30	434	101	13.1	.341	2.2	CF(72): 7.9, RF(29): 0.4	2.5
2017	KCA	MLB	31	645	119	36.6	.340	2.4	CF(151): 19.4	6.0
2018	MIL	MLB	32	620	121	52.9	.357	4.3	CF(138): 2.1	4.5
2019	MIL	MLB	33	634	112	37.6	.329	2.8	CF 10	4.7

Lorenzo Cain, continued

Batted Ball Distribution

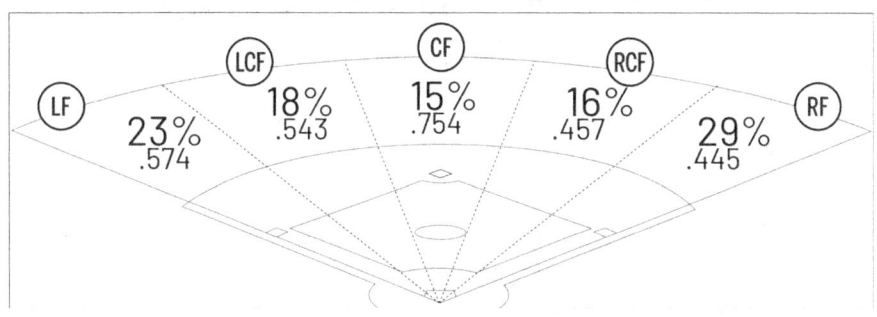

Strike Zone vs LHP

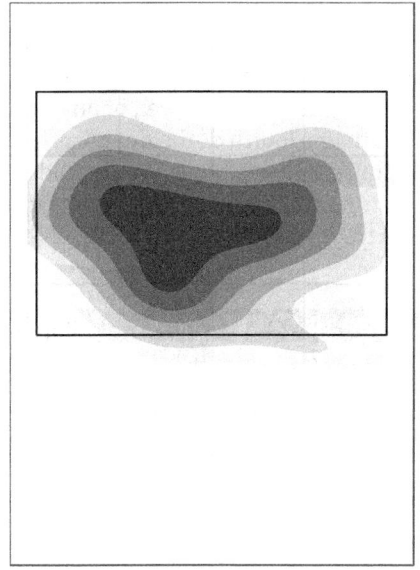

Strike Zone vs RHP

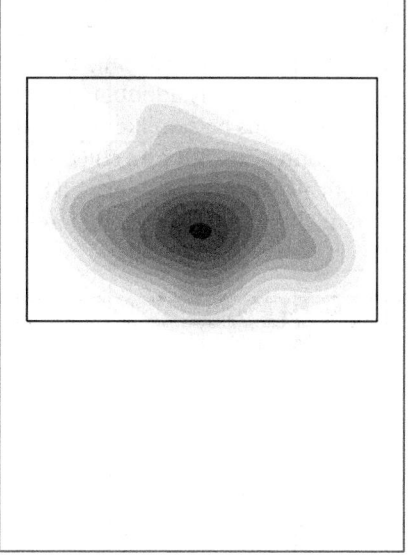

Milwaukee Brewers 2019

Ben Gamel LF

Born: 05/17/92   Age: 27   Bats: L   Throws: L
Height: 5'11"   Weight: 185   Origin: Round 10, 2010 Draft (#325 overall)

YEAR	TEAM	LVL	AGE	PA	R	2B	3B	HR	RBI	BB	K	SB	CS	AVG/OBP/SLG
2016	NYA	MLB	24	10	1	0	0	0	0	1	1	0	0	.125/.222/.125
2016	SWB	AAA	24	533	80	26	5	6	51	43	94	19	8	.308/.365/.420
2016	SEA	MLB	24	47	8	2	0	1	5	5	15	0	0	.200/.289/.325
2017	TAC	AAA	25	75	6	1	1	1	8	12	11	1	1	.300/.427/.400
2017	SEA	MLB	25	550	68	27	5	11	59	36	122	4	1	.275/.322/.413
2018	TAC	AAA	26	94	19	8	3	1	16	10	12	4	0	.349/.415/.554
2018	SEA	MLB	26	293	37	14	4	1	19	31	61	7	3	.272/.358/.370
2019	MIL	MLB	27	300	34	13	2	6	30	27	65	5	2	.260/.330/.390

Breakout: 8%   Improve: 45%   Collapse: 14%   Attrition: 18%   MLB: 93%
Comparables: Matt Murton, Robbie Grossman, Andy Dirks

Rebounding from a disastrous second half in 2017, Gamel proved that he may indeed be a useful big leaguer. While his offensive contributions still rely more on the dark, fickle magic of BABIP than one would like, he nearly doubled his walk rate in 2018 and maintained his mysterious fielder-avoiding hitting skills. Not particularly fast, or strong-armed, Gamel's instincts and aggressiveness make him a perfectly adequate corner outfielder. His lack of power, or any true plus skill, means he's unlikely anything more than a fourth outfielder on a playoff contender, but he's still only 26. His frame and raw power tool would theoretically allow for more; he'll have fewer opportunities to demonstrate it this year after the Brewers obtained him in a trade to fill their fourth-outfielder role.

YEAR	TEAM	LVL	AGE	PA	DRC+	VORP	BABIP	BRR	FRAA	WARP
2016	NYA	MLB	24	10	71	-0.4	.143	0.2	RF(5): -0.5	0.0
2016	SWB	AAA	24	533	126	34.1	.370	4.6	CF(70): -7.3, LF(25): 0.3	1.9
2016	SEA	MLB	24	47	69	0.5	.292	0.1	RF(24): -1.5, LF(2): -0.4	-0.2
2017	TAC	AAA	25	75	117	5.9	.347	0.6	RF(11): -0.2, CF(7): -0.9	0.2
2017	SEA	MLB	25	550	90	13.3	.340	1.1	LF(85): -3.5, RF(50): 3.1	0.7
2018	TAC	AAA	26	94	136	10.7	.394	2.5	LF(8): -0.7, CF(6): -0.1	0.6
2018	SEA	MLB	26	293	98	12.4	.352	3.3	LF(48): -1.4, RF(40): -1.9	0.7
2019	MIL	MLB	27	300	95	8.7	.325	0.2	RF -2, LF -1	0.4

Ben Gamel, continued

Batted Ball Distribution

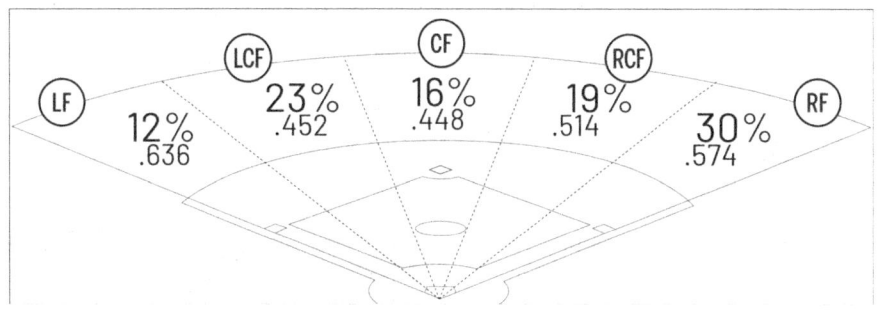

Strike Zone vs LHP

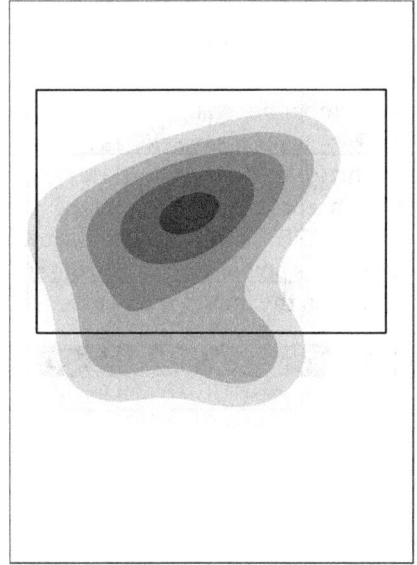

Strike Zone vs RHP

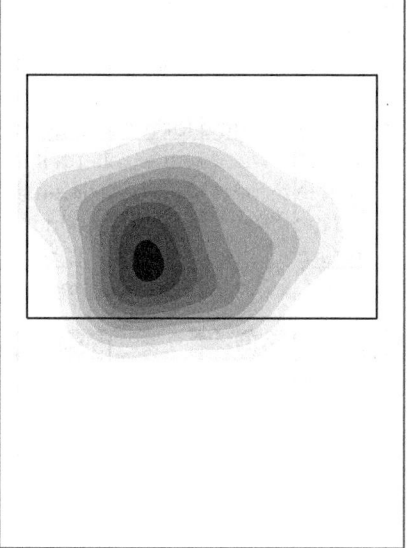

Milwaukee Brewers 2019

Yasmani Grandal C

Born: 11/08/88   Age: 30   Bats: B   Throws: R
Height: 6'1"   Weight: 235   Origin: Round 1, 2010 Draft (#12 overall)

YEAR	TEAM	LVL	AGE	PA	R	2B	3B	HR	RBI	BB	K	SB	CS	AVG/OBP/SLG
2016	LAN	MLB	27	457	49	14	1	27	72	64	116	1	3	.228/.339/.477
2017	LAN	MLB	28	482	50	27	0	22	58	40	130	0	1	.247/.308/.459
2018	LAN	MLB	29	518	65	23	2	24	68	72	124	2	1	.241/.349/.466
2019	MIL	MLB	30	476	57	20	2	19	63	53	122	1	1	.237/.326/.432

Breakout: 4%   Improve: 35%   Collapse: 8%   Attrition: 9%   MLB: 97%
Comparables: Geovany Soto, Chris Iannetta, Miguel Montero

If you're wondering about big talent experiencing bumps in the road, always remember, James Cameron directed Piranha Part Two: The Spawning. And just like that sequel, Grandal's post-season once again burst into flames like a trash-filled dumpster.

YEAR	TEAM	P. COUNT	FRM RUNS	BLK RUNS	THRW RUNS	TOT RUNS
2016	LAN	15887	28.0	0.3	0.5	29.2
2017	LAN	16211	26.2	-1.4	1.3	26.2
2018	LAN	16615	15.7	0.8	0.1	16.3
2019	MIL	15871	22.2	-0.3	0.6	22.5

This year's nightmare extended to both sides of the ball, with uncharacteristic defensive miscues piling on top of terrible at-bats. The combination again led to an unceremonious October benching, this one at the worst possible time for the free-agent-to-be. Recency bias now clouds the fact that Grandal was again excellent, if inconsistent, for the boys in blue; He checked in as baseball's best defensive catcher according to FRAA, and the second most valuable backstop in the game by WARP. His easy double-digit walk rate returned after a brief hiatus, along with his plus power. Ultimately, the stick is a bonus, as Grandal makes his box office bank on the merits of that defense.

YEAR	TEAM	LVL	AGE	PA	DRC+	VORP	BABIP	BRR	FRAA	WARP
2016	LAN	MLB	27	457	115	33.1	.250	-5.1	C(115): 33.2, 1B(4): 0.4	6.0
2017	LAN	MLB	28	482	93	25.8	.298	-2.6	C(117): 27.7	4.5
2018	LAN	MLB	29	518	113	36.1	.278	-4.4	C(135): 17.7, 1B(2): 0.0	4.7
2019	MIL	MLB	30	476	100	19.1	.285	-1.0	C 22	4.2

Yasmani Grandal, continued

Batted Ball Distribution

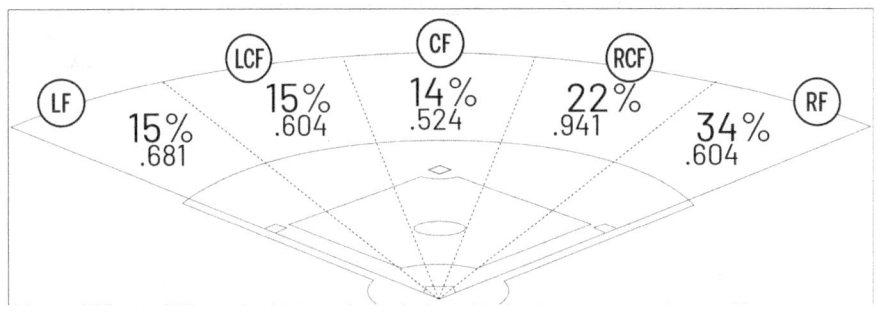

Strike Zone vs LHP   **Strike Zone vs RHP**

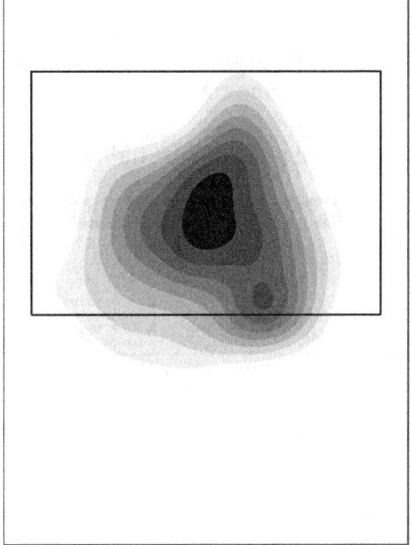

Mike Moustakas 3B

Born: 09/11/88 Age: 30 Bats: L Throws: R
Height: 6'0" Weight: 225 Origin: Round 1, 2007 Draft (#2 overall)

YEAR	TEAM	LVL	AGE	PA	R	2B	3B	HR	RBI	BB	K	SB	CS	AVG/OBP/SLG
2016	KCA	MLB	27	113	12	6	0	7	13	9	13	0	1	.240/.301/.500
2017	KCA	MLB	28	598	75	24	0	38	85	34	94	0	0	.272/.314/.521
2018	KCA	MLB	29	417	46	21	1	20	62	30	63	3	0	.249/.309/.468
2018	MIL	MLB	29	218	20	12	0	8	33	19	40	1	1	.256/.326/.441
2019	MIL	MLB	30	525	68	25	2	25	78	43	89	2	1	.270/.334/.489

Breakout: 2% Improve: 36% Collapse: 21% Attrition: 9% MLB: 95%
Comparables: Kyle Seager, Aubrey Huff, Garrett Atkins

From one small-market champion to another upstart contender, Moustakas had the opportunity to add a new line to his resume in 2018. The former Royals champion third baseman became a valuable midseason acquisition for the plucky Brewers, perhaps the veteran leadership profile for the Ivy League Analytics Age. That calling card power showed once again, and it was enough to carry the veteran's profile even if it was slightly diminished from a 2017 home run breakout. Moustakas is the type of productive player who can fade to a supporting role while doing just about everything right; this arrangement works because nothing categorically stands out among the walks, strikeouts, extra-base hits and glove. It's all there, enough to acquire Moustakas for a contending season and plug into the fifth or sixth batting spot.

YEAR	TEAM	LVL	AGE	PA	DRC+	VORP	BABIP	BRR	FRAA	WARP
2016	KCA	MLB	27	113	121	5.4	.214	-0.7	3B(26): -0.4	0.6
2017	KCA	MLB	28	598	121	26.5	.263	-1.6	3B(127): -7.4	2.7
2018	KCA	MLB	29	417	109	14.2	.247	-2.6	3B(76): 11.3, 1B(4): -0.2	2.7
2018	MIL	MLB	29	218	107	8.0	.282	-2.6	3B(52): 0.5	0.8
2019	MIL	MLB	30	525	114	24.9	.283	-0.8	2B 0, 3B 0	2.6

Mike Moustakas, continued

Batted Ball Distribution

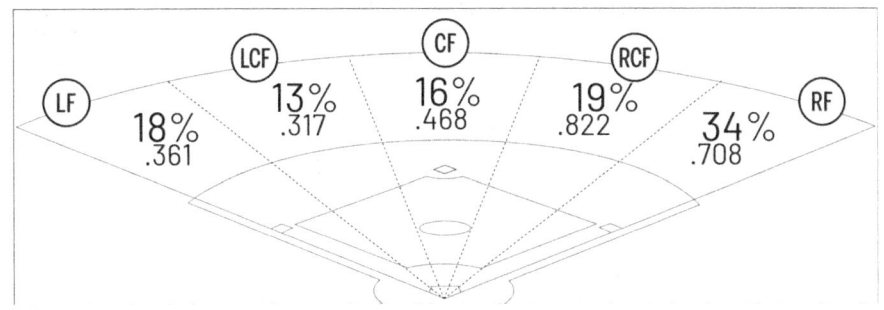

Strike Zone vs LHP

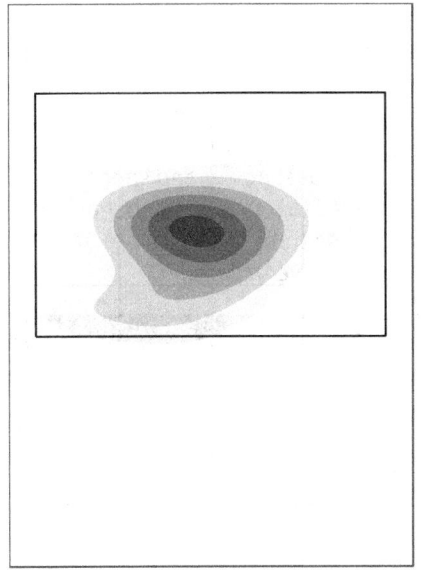

Strike Zone vs RHP

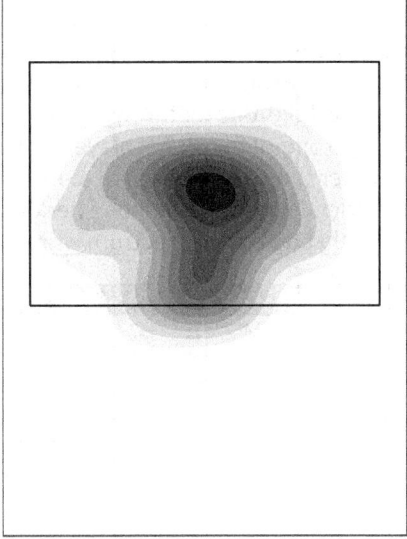

Hernan Perez UT

Born: 03/26/91 Age: 28 Bats: R Throws: R
Height: 6'1" Weight: 215 Origin: International Free Agent, 2007

YEAR	TEAM	LVL	AGE	PA	R	2B	3B	HR	RBI	BB	K	SB	CS	AVG/OBP/SLG
2016	CSP	AAA	25	67	10	4	1	1	11	3	10	2	0	.339/.364/.484
2016	MIL	MLB	25	430	50	18	3	13	56	18	94	34	7	.272/.302/.428
2017	MIL	MLB	26	458	47	19	3	14	51	20	79	13	4	.259/.289/.414
2018	MIL	MLB	27	334	36	11	2	9	29	17	71	11	3	.253/.290/.386
2019	MIL	MLB	28	295	35	13	2	8	33	17	59	12	3	.260/.306/.410

Breakout: 4% Improve: 54% Collapse: 11% Attrition: 20% MLB: 93%
Comparables: Brandon Phillips, Tyler Saladino, Scooter Gennett

"If you can play shortstop, you can play anywhere" is a relatively common utterance on broadcasts, whispered in hushed tones befitting of a rumor so mundane as to be unquestionably true. Perez pushes this rumor to the extreme and is therefore a singular player. Whereas some might take an entire career to make those moves away from shortstop, down the defensive spectrum to third base, perhaps second base, maybe the outfield and first base, Perez makes those moves during a single season. According to the Baseball-Reference Play Index, Perez is the only player in recorded history to play 20 games each at 2B, 3B, SS and RF in one season. This level of sustained flexibility deserves analytical scrutiny for throwing the defensive spectrum into a blender. Perez is hardly a one-dimensional player either, as his modest power and speed makes his other shortcomings easier to forget. Piece it all together and a manager's best friend emerges, someone perfect for grinding through 162 games, up and down that defensive spectrum whenever and however it calls.

YEAR	TEAM	LVL	AGE	PA	DRC+	VORP	BABIP	BRR	FRAA	WARP
2016	CSP	AAA	25	67	108	4.4	.385	0.4	2B(10): -0.8, 3B(6): 0.1	0.1
2016	MIL	MLB	25	430	92	19.8	.322	3.0	3B(60): -0.5, RF(36): 3.6	1.5
2017	MIL	MLB	26	458	83	9.4	.286	2.4	LF(53): 2.5, 3B(31): 3.4	1.0
2018	MIL	MLB	27	334	92	9.7	.300	0.6	2B(51): -0.9, RF(27): 0.4	0.7
2019	MIL	MLB	28	295	89	7.4	.298	1.4	SS -1, 2B -1	0.6

Hernan Perez, continued

Batted Ball Distribution

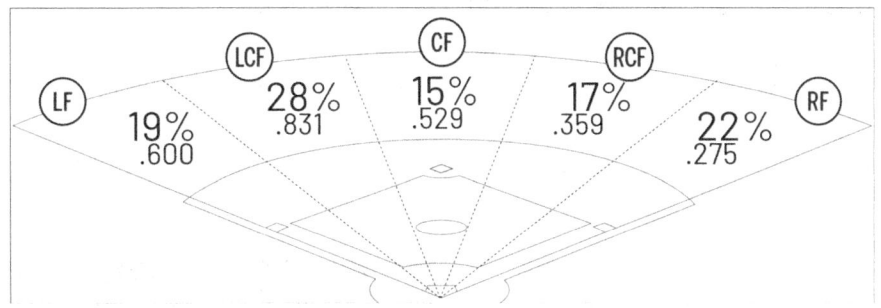

Strike Zone vs LHP

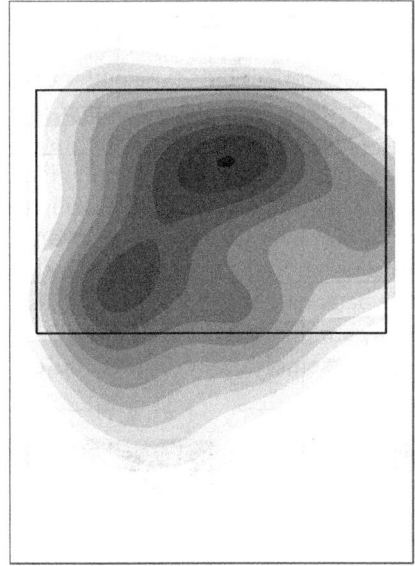

Strike Zone vs RHP

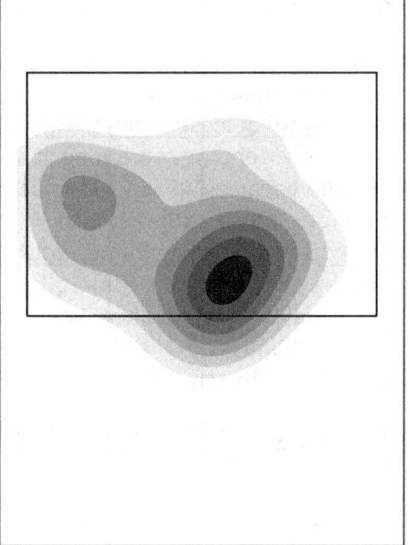

Manny Pina C

Born: 06/05/87 Age: 32 Bats: R Throws: R
Height: 6'0" Weight: 215 Origin: International Free Agent, 2004

YEAR	TEAM	LVL	AGE	PA	R	2B	3B	HR	RBI	BB	K	SB	CS	AVG/OBP/SLG
2016	CSP	AAA	29	262	35	21	3	5	43	17	39	1	1	.329/.371/.506
2016	MIL	MLB	29	81	4	4	0	2	12	10	15	0	1	.254/.346/.394
2017	MIL	MLB	30	359	45	21	0	9	43	20	79	2	0	.279/.327/.424
2018	MIL	MLB	31	337	39	13	2	9	28	21	62	2	0	.252/.307/.395
2019	MIL	MLB	32	96	10	5	0	2	10	7	20	0	0	.253/.312/.379

Breakout: 2% Improve: 26% Collapse: 17% Attrition: 15% MLB: 83%
Comparables: Ronny Paulino, John Baker, Miguel Ojeda

The ostensible goal of a baseball season is to win as many games as possible, but the most effective manner of reaching that goal is debatable. Rather than outscoring an opponent as frequently as possible, which would be a clearly acceptable objective for winning frequently, a team can also work to bide time better than their opponents. For much of baseball is waiting for something to happen, to effectively (or at least competently) fill in the gaps while both teams are waiting for that never-ending something. It's why the sport can withstand profiles like Pina, who began as an age-29 rookie catcher by hitting just enough, walking a bit and playing passable defense. That profile may eventually morph into an age-31 catcher who can frame, block and throw, emerging as one of the best defensive catchers in the game, all the while balancing that line by hitting just enough. Value does not always need to loudly announce itself via big WARP and loud tools. Pina is not the big moment, but he assembles value in every little moment in-between.

YEAR	TEAM	P. COUNT	FRM RUNS	BLK RUNS	THRW RUNS	TOT RUNS
2016	MIL	2273	-0.5	-0.2	-0.1	-0.6
2017	MIL	12774	-2.9	0.7	2.0	3.0
2018	MIL	12411	4.8	1.3	0.5	6.3
2019	MIL	3581	-0.4	0.2	0.2	0.0

YEAR	TEAM	LVL	AGE	PA	DRC+	VORP	BABIP	BRR	FRAA	WARP
2016	CSP	AAA	29	262	121	17.8	.371	-3.4	C(57): -7.7	0.2
2016	MIL	MLB	29	81	96	2.4	.296	-1.2	C(17): -0.8	0.1
2017	MIL	MLB	30	359	93	16.8	.339	-0.6	C(102): 1.4	1.5
2018	MIL	MLB	31	337	90	8.8	.285	-3.6	C(92): 7.0, 1B(1): 0.0	1.6
2019	MIL	MLB	32	96	87	2.6	.304	-0.1	C -1	0.2

Manny Pina, continued

Batted Ball Distribution

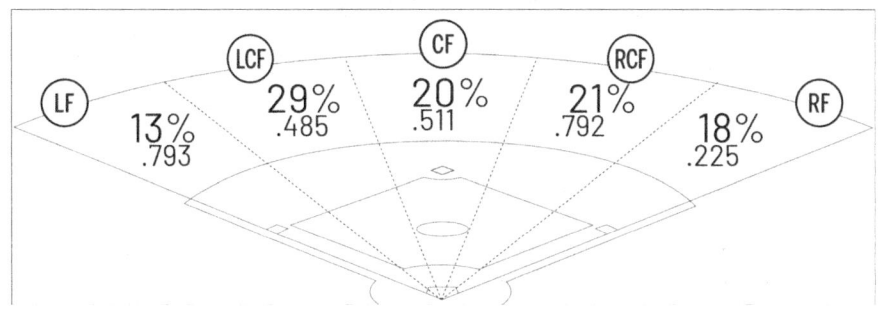

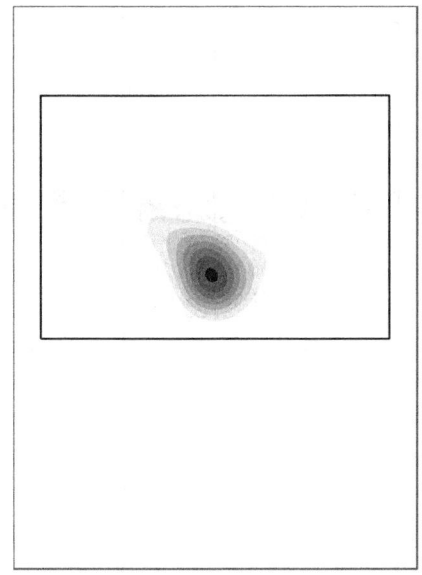

Strike Zone vs LHP

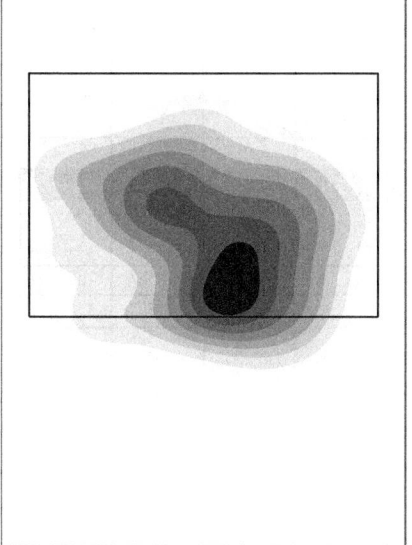

Strike Zone vs RHP

Travis Shaw INF

Born: 04/16/90 Age: 29 Bats: L Throws: R
Height: 6'4" Weight: 230 Origin: Round 9, 2011 Draft (#292 overall)

YEAR	TEAM	LVL	AGE	PA	R	2B	3B	HR	RBI	BB	K	SB	CS	AVG/OBP/SLG
2016	BOS	MLB	26	530	63	34	2	16	71	43	133	5	1	.242/.306/.421
2017	MIL	MLB	27	606	84	34	1	31	101	60	138	10	0	.273/.349/.513
2018	MIL	MLB	28	587	73	23	0	32	86	78	108	5	2	.241/.345/.480
2019	MIL	MLB	29	488	63	24	2	21	68	50	108	5	1	.260/.341/.472

Breakout: 2%   Improve: 41%   Collapse: 11%   Attrition: 11%   MLB: 99%
Comparables: Chase Headley, Todd Frazier, Eric Chavez

If there were an award for Process-Oriented Vanguard, Shaw would be one of the frontrunners. The big third baseman tested fan perception of surface stats throughout the season, as the batting average (and, sometimes, slugging results) seemed to suggest a regression. Yet Shaw sliced his strikeout totals by roughly 20 percent, increased the walks, shredded line drives and lifted more batted balls into the air. Meanwhile in the field, the prototypical 3B-to-1B defensive spectrum prospect became the face of the Brewers' unorthodox defensive arrangements, willingly becoming a second baseman in Milwaukee's aggressive shifts once the club acquired Mike Moustakas. Thus the Vanguard, of fly balls, shifts and walks, Shaw represents one particularly intriguing mutation of MLB success.

YEAR	TEAM	LVL	AGE	PA	DRC+	VORP	BABIP	BRR	FRAA	WARP
2016	BOS	MLB	26	530	88	5.7	.299	-0.8	3B(105): 7.4, 1B(50): 2.3	1.8
2017	MIL	MLB	27	606	114	41.5	.312	3.2	3B(143): 0.9, 1B(1): 0.0	3.7
2018	MIL	MLB	28	587	120	42.9	.242	-0.7	3B(107): 1.8, 2B(39): -0.5	3.5
2019	MIL	MLB	29	488	111	19.0	.297	-0.2	3B 3	2.1

Travis Shaw, continued

Batted Ball Distribution

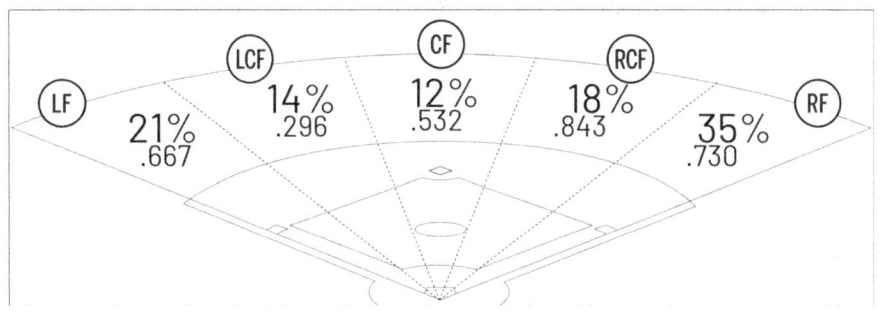

Strike Zone vs LHP

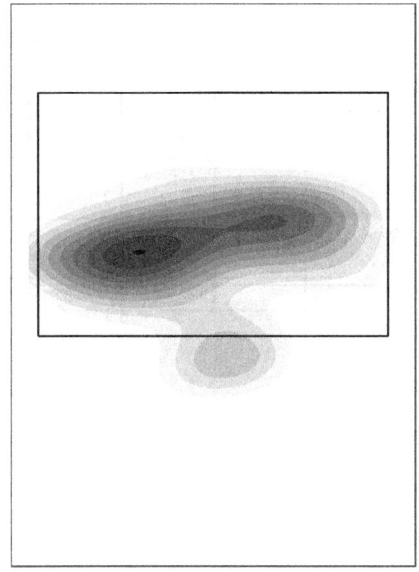

Strike Zone vs RHP

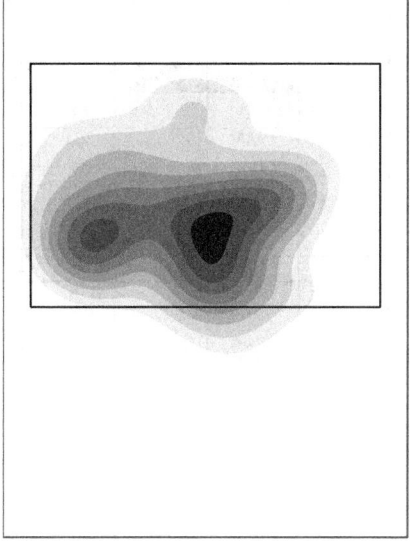

Cory Spangenberg 2B

Born: 03/16/91 Age: 28 Bats: L Throws: R
Height: 6'0" Weight: 195 Origin: Round 1, 2011 Draft (#10 overall)

YEAR	TEAM	LVL	AGE	PA	R	2B	3B	HR	RBI	BB	K	SB	CS	AVG/OBP/SLG
2016	SDN	MLB	25	53	6	1	1	1	8	4	13	1	0	.229/.302/.354
2017	ELP	AAA	26	72	8	3	1	1	7	4	8	3	2	.348/.403/.470
2017	SDN	MLB	26	486	57	18	2	13	46	34	128	11	3	.264/.322/.401
2018	ELP	AAA	27	95	14	8	2	4	16	6	30	3	0	.341/.383/.614
2018	SDN	MLB	27	329	35	9	4	7	25	25	108	6	1	.235/.298/.362
2019	MIL	MLB	28	188	22	7	1	5	20	15	51	4	1	.244/.312/.387

Breakout: 8% Improve: 48% Collapse: 13% Attrition: 17% MLB: 95%
Comparables: Jayson Nix, Trevor Plouffe, Josh Rutledge

Spangenberg has never done anything particularly well or badly, which more or less makes him the face of the franchise. He keeps hanging around, like a couch that's so ugly everyone just assumes it's comfortable, starting more often than not and whelming with inoffensive and unspectacular play. He's been a fine placeholder at second, but presuming that Luis Urias hits, Spangenberg will likely anchor the lineup for some other rebuilding club sooner rather than later.

YEAR	TEAM	LVL	AGE	PA	DRC+	VORP	BABIP	BRR	FRAA	WARP
2016	SDN	MLB	25	53	69	-0.2	.294	-0.2	2B(13): 0.4	0.0
2017	ELP	AAA	26	72	104	3.3	.386	-0.2	3B(17): -3.3	-0.1
2017	SDN	MLB	26	486	82	28.6	.342	5.3	3B(96): -0.8, LF(32): -3.0	0.8
2018	ELP	AAA	27	95	117	6.4	.481	-0.4	3B(13): 0.8, 2B(5): -0.9	0.3
2018	SDN	MLB	27	329	64	4.3	.344	-0.1	2B(49): -2.8, 3B(44): 0.3	-0.7
2019	MIL	MLB	28	188	80	2.3	.312	0.4	2B -1, 3B 0	0.1

Cory Spangenberg, continued

Batted Ball Distribution

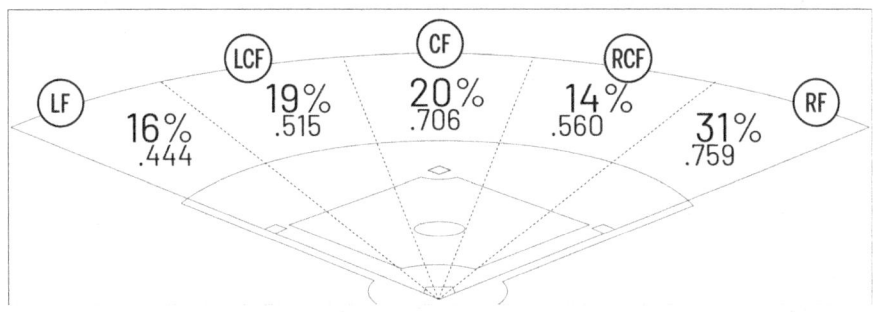

Strike Zone vs LHP   **Strike Zone vs RHP**

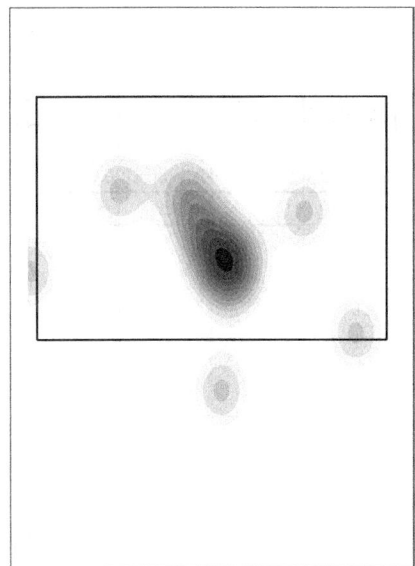
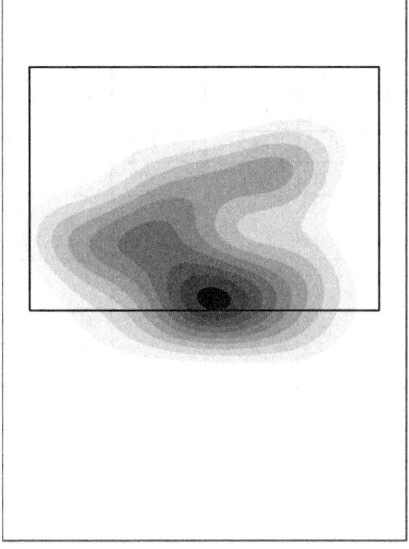

Eric Thames 1B

Born: 11/10/86 Age: 32 Bats: L Throws: R
Height: 6'0" Weight: 210 Origin: Round 7, 2008 Draft (#219 overall)

YEAR	TEAM	LVL	AGE	PA	R	2B	3B	HR	RBI	BB	K	SB	CS	AVG/OBP/SLG
2017	MIL	MLB	30	551	83	26	4	31	63	75	163	4	2	.247/.359/.518
2018	MIL	MLB	31	278	41	10	3	16	37	29	97	7	0	.219/.306/.478
2019	MIL	MLB	32	300	39	14	2	13	42	32	95	4	1	.243/.330/.460

Breakout: 0% Improve: 18% Collapse: 24% Attrition: 8% MLB: 100%
Comparables: Mike Napoli, Richie Sexson, Fred McGriff

Three True Outcomes, no waiting. Thames' massive power remained in his second season back from Korea, but his walks went down and his strikeouts went up, leaving him with a much lesser role for the Brewers. Among all left-handed hitters with at least 500 plate appearances in 2017-2018, his .267 isolated power ranked second to only Joey Gallo, but he also whiffed in a higher percentage of his at-bats than all lefties except Gallo, Chris Davis and Alex Avila. Thames' likely 2019 output is probably somewhere in between, but the Brewers may no longer need his strengths enough to live with more than 300-400 plate appearances of his weaknesses.

YEAR	TEAM	LVL	AGE	PA	DRC+	VORP	BABIP	BRR	FRAA	WARP
2017	MIL	MLB	30	551	117	29.5	.309	-2.7	1B(108): -2.2, LF(25): -1.8	1.4
2018	MIL	MLB	31	278	96	13.7	.284	2.3	RF(31): -0.3, 1B(29): -0.9	0.6
2019	MIL	MLB	32	300	104	8.9	.318	0.2	1B 0, LF 0	1.0

Eric Thames, continued

Batted Ball Distribution

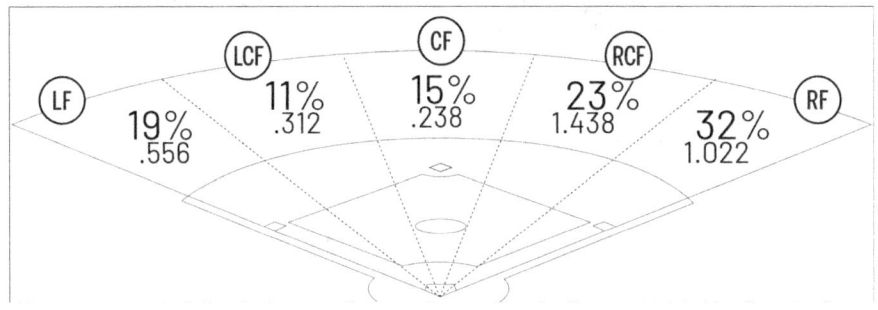

Strike Zone vs LHP

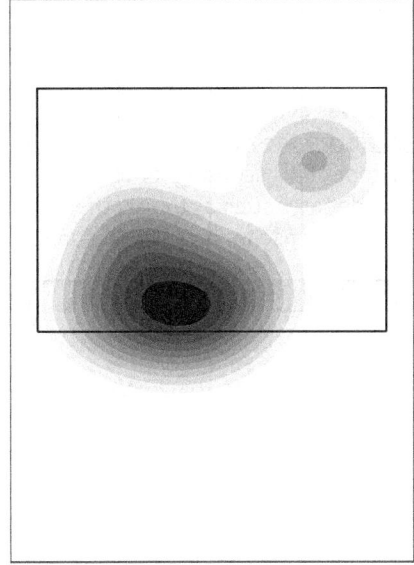

Strike Zone vs RHP

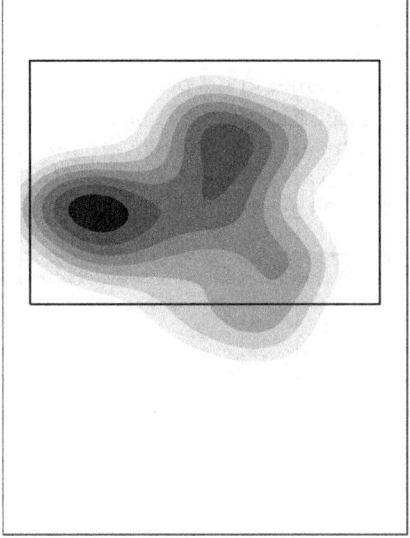

Milwaukee Brewers 2019

Christian Yelich LF

Born: 12/05/91 Age: 27 Bats: L Throws: R
Height: 6'3" Weight: 195 Origin: Round 1, 2010 Draft (#23 overall)

YEAR	TEAM	LVL	AGE	PA	R	2B	3B	HR	RBI	BB	K	SB	CS	AVG/OBP/SLG
2016	MIA	MLB	24	659	78	38	3	21	98	72	138	9	4	.298/.376/.483
2017	MIA	MLB	25	695	100	36	2	18	81	80	137	16	2	.282/.369/.439
2018	MIL	MLB	26	651	118	34	7	36	110	68	135	22	4	.326/.402/.598
2019	MIL	MLB	27	659	99	32	4	25	81	67	143	16	4	.284/.363/.481

Breakout: 8%   Improve: 48%   Collapse: 13%   Attrition: 6%   MLB: 93%
Comparables: Oscar Gamble, Enos Slaughter, Nick Markakis

During the playoffs, the *Los Angeles Times* reported that Yelich worked on several aspects of his offseason conditioning, and also lifted weights throughout the season for the first time in his career. When the closing bell rang on the first half, Yelich boasted a .292/.364/.459 line, a perfectly respectable debut in Milwaukee and a reasonable extension of his previous seasons in Miami. Yelich paired those physical tweaks with improved plate discipline throughout the second half, which catapulted the flexible outfielder into the MVP debate. It was evident during the last two weeks of July, when Yelich opened the second half with 12 extra-base hits in 12 games, it was evident in August when Yelich went deep 11 times in 124 plate appearances and it was evident when Yelich leveled up to lead the Brewers' unbelievable stretch run for the NL Central crown. The smooth-swinging bat unlocked the fullest extent of his scouting report, leaving potential areas of improvement for academic debates such as the aesthetics of a 1.000 OPS or whether Yelich can play right field defense for an entire season.

YEAR	TEAM	LVL	AGE	PA	DRC+	VORP	BABIP	BRR	FRAA	WARP
2016	MIA	MLB	24	659	114	56.6	.356	2.2	LF(120): -5.0, CF(31): 0.0	2.6
2017	MIA	MLB	25	695	105	46.3	.336	0.8	CF(155): -17.3	1.2
2018	MIL	MLB	26	651	143	78.0	.373	2.4	LF(90): -7.3, RF(75): 2.1	4.8
2019	MIL	MLB	27	659	123	40.1	.336	1.5	RF 4, CF -1	4.1

Christian Yelich, continued

Batted Ball Distribution

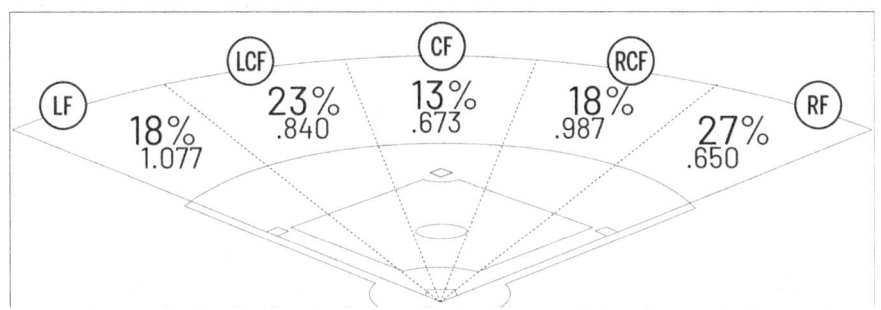

Strike Zone vs LHP

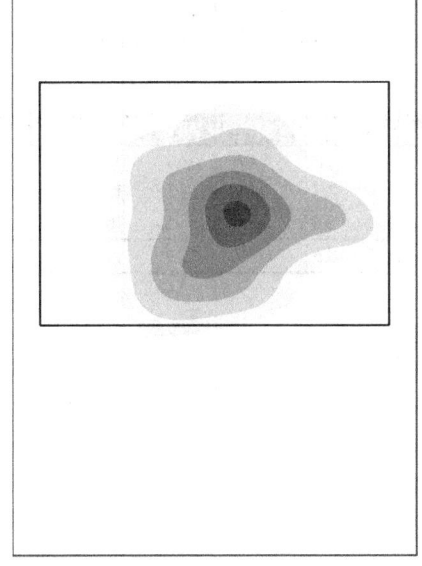

Strike Zone vs RHP

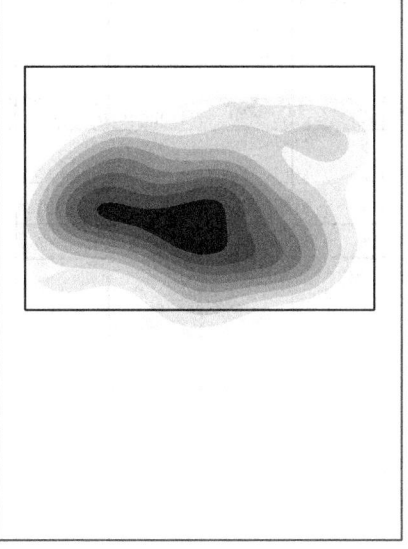

Milwaukee Brewers 2019

Chase Anderson   RHP
Born: 11/30/87   Age: 31   Bats: R   Throws: R
Height: 6'1"   Weight: 200   Origin: Round 9, 2009 Draft (#276 overall)

YEAR	TEAM	LVL	AGE	W	L	SV	G	GS	IP	H	HR	BB/9	K/9	K	GB%	BABIP
2016	MIL	MLB	28	9	11	0	31	30	151[2]	155	28	3.1	7.1	120	38%	.287
2017	MIL	MLB	29	12	4	0	25	25	141[1]	113	14	2.6	8.5	133	41%	.265
2018	MIL	MLB	30	9	8	0	30	30	158	131	30	3.2	7.3	128	36%	.239
2019	MIL	MLB	31	9	8	0	25	25	142	131	21	3.0	8.4	133	39%	.283

Breakout: 19%   Improve: 51%   Collapse: 17%   Attrition: 14%   MLB: 87%
Comparables: Jeremy Hellickson, Jeff Francis, Brian Bannister

The righty was inexplicably shut down during the Brewers' white-hot run in September despite a 15-start stretch featuring a strikeout-to-walk ratio near 3-to-1 and just 28 runs allowed in 77 innings. Anderson struggled with command and velocity vultures all season, as the fastball dipped below 93 mph during several months while demonstrating some monthly fluctuation patterns similar to 2017. Into August and September, Anderson sandwiched good and bad starts, placing a downward trend on that strong 15-start stretch and adding to the frustration of a season that never seemed bad but never delivered on the promise of the prior year's glory.

YEAR	TEAM	LVL	AGE	WHIP	ERA	DRA	WARP	MPH	FB%	WHF	CSP
2016	MIL	MLB	28	1.37	4.39	5.34	0.0	93.6	56.7	9.2	46.9
2017	MIL	MLB	29	1.09	2.74	4.13	2.3	94.9	52.5	11.5	47.6
2018	MIL	MLB	30	1.19	3.93	5.52	-0.4	94.1	53.5	10.3	46.9
2019	MIL	MLB	31	1.23	4.21	4.70	0.6	93.4	53.7	10.3	46.9

Chase Anderson, continued

Pitch Shape vs LHH

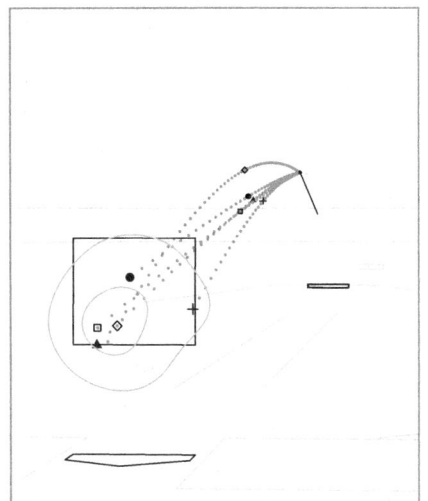

Pitch Shape vs RHH

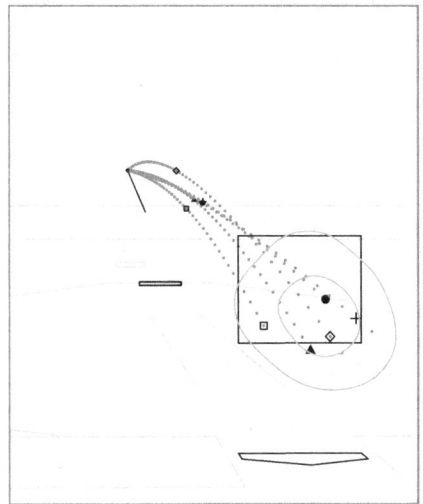

Type		Frequency	Velocity	H Movement	V Movement
●	Fastball	40.8%	92.9 [101]	-6.8 [100]	-13.2 [108]
□	Sinker	12.6%	92.3 [99]	-12.2 [103]	-16.7 [112]
+	Cutter	9.9%	89.1 [102]	2.8 [105]	-20.3 [114]
▲	Changeup	18.7%	82.6 [89]	-14.6 [82]	-26 [104]
×	Splitter				
▽	Slider				
◇	Curveball	17.9%	77.1 [95]	7.6 [99]	-52.4 [90]
⊕	Slow Curveball				
✳	Knuckleball				
▼	Screwball				

Corbin Burnes RHP

Born: 10/22/94 Age: 24 Bats: R Throws: R
Height: 6'3" Weight: 205 Origin: Round 4, 2016 Draft (#111 overall)

YEAR	TEAM	LVL	AGE	W	L	SV	G	GS	IP	H	HR	BB/9	K/9	K	GB%	BABIP
2016	BRR	RK	21	0	0	0	3	1	7	3	0	2.6	12.9	10	64%	.214
2016	WIS	A	21	3	0	0	9	5	28²	20	1	5.0	9.7	31	64%	.275
2017	CAR	A+	22	5	0	0	10	10	60	37	1	2.4	8.4	56	54%	.243
2017	BLX	AA	22	3	3	0	16	16	85²	66	2	2.1	8.8	84	51%	.279
2018	CSP	AAA	23	3	4	0	19	13	78²	83	7	3.5	9.3	81	47%	.347
2018	MIL	MLB	23	7	0	1	30	0	38	27	4	2.6	8.3	35	50%	.232
2019	MIL	MLB	24	5	4	0	32	11	77	70	10	4.1	9.1	79	48%	.290

Breakout: 20% Improve: 41% Collapse: 20% Attrition: 25% MLB: 76%
Comparables: Robbie Ross, Nick Tropeano, Alex Cobb

Judging Burnes strictly by age, height and weight for his rookie season, one of the comps is Michael Fulmer. Burnes spent most of 2017 ramping up his stuff at a rate that seemed nearly impossible for evaluators to catch up; at each different locale, he seemed to offer something different. Fulmer followed a similar path as a surefire mid-rotation pitcher turned quasi-ace, and Burnes flashed signs of that brilliant potential in a bullpen stint with Milwaukee. But the bullpen will likely not be home for Burnes, who can no longer keep his hard-driving 96 mph fastball and two breaking pitches a secret.

YEAR	TEAM	LVL	AGE	WHIP	ERA	DRA	WARP	MPH	FB%	WHF	CSP
2016	BRR	RK	21	0.71	1.29	2.74	0.2				
2016	WIS	A	21	1.26	2.20	3.91	0.3				
2017	CAR	A+	22	0.88	1.05	4.48	0.5				
2017	BLX	AA	22	1.00	2.10	2.97	2.2				
2018	CSP	AAA	23	1.45	5.15	3.52	1.8				
2018	MIL	MLB	23	1.00	2.61	3.39	0.7	97.0	58.8	15.8	50.6
2019	MIL	MLB	24	1.35	4.26	4.70	0.3	96.8	60.6	16.2	52.1

Corbin Burnes, continued

Pitch Shape vs LHH

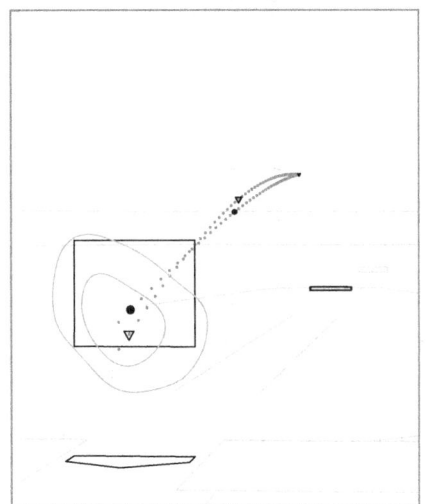

Pitch Shape vs RHH

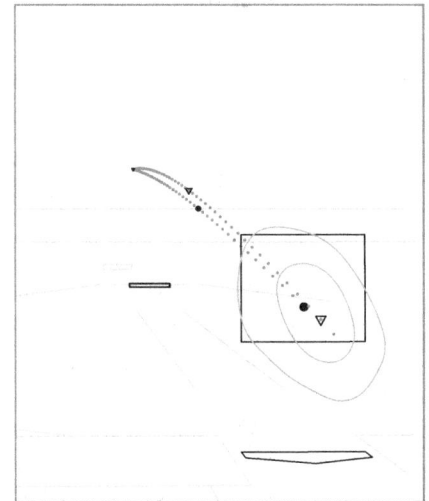

Type	Frequency	Velocity	H Movement	V Movement
● Fastball	58.7%	95.8 [110]	-0.7 [128]	-14.9 [103]
☐ Sinker	0.2%	96.7 [121]	-12.9 [98]	-17.3 [110]
+ Cutter				
▲ Changeup	0.2%	88.2 [111]	-5.2 [132]	-31.8 [87]
✕ Splitter				
▽ Slider	34.2%	87.1 [112]	5.6 [103]	-31.3 [105]
◇ Curveball	6.8%	80.3 [107]	10.4 [111]	-45 [107]
✦ Slow Curveball				
✴ Knuckleball				
▼ Screwball				

Brewers Player Analysis - 49

Jhoulys Chacin   RHP

Born: 01/07/88   Age: 31   Bats: R   Throws: R
Height: 6'3"   Weight: 215   Origin: International Free Agent, 2004

YEAR	TEAM	LVL	AGE	W	L	SV	G	GS	IP	H	HR	BB/9	K/9	K	GB%	BABIP
2016	GWN	AAA	28	1	0	0	1	1	7²	5	0	2.3	8.2	7	53%	.263
2016	ATL	MLB	28	1	2	0	5	5	26²	29	4	2.7	9.1	27	50%	.321
2016	ANA	MLB	28	5	6	0	29	17	117¹	124	10	3.6	7.1	92	52%	.316
2017	SDN	MLB	29	13	10	0	32	32	180¹	157	19	3.6	7.6	153	50%	.272
2018	MIL	MLB	30	15	8	0	35	35	192²	153	18	3.3	7.3	156	44%	.250
2019	MIL	MLB	31	11	10	0	30	30	171	154	22	3.3	8.4	160	46%	.282

Breakout: 14%   Improve: 40%   Collapse: 22%   Attrition: 13%   MLB: 88%
Comparables: Tanner Roark, Andrew Cashner, Scott Feldman

Everything wiggles; Chacin throws nothing flat. If you're watching him, look for a looping slider that defies definition of any breaking ball you know. In an era when so many pitchers insist on working hard velocity and sharp, darting sliders, Chacin's slider seems to chug up to the plate and bend in the same manner as its author dances on the mound. You'd dance, too, if you were a dependable, unsung rotation worker signed early during an austerity offseason, celebrating your success as opposed to so many more obvious free agent choices to boost a potential contender. It doesn't always work for the righty, and if you didn't want to have any fun you could write a book about his shortcomings, but none of that matters when Game 163 is on the line, or even some playoff games. Chacin dances like the ace you didn't know you needed.

YEAR	TEAM	LVL	AGE	WHIP	ERA	DRA	WARP	MPH	FB%	WHF	CSP
2016	GWN	AAA	28	0.91	0.00	2.90	0.2				
2016	ATL	MLB	28	1.39	5.40	3.19	0.6	92.4	55.1	11.6	46.3
2016	ANA	MLB	28	1.46	4.68	5.27	0.0	93.9	55.1	8.1	47.5
2017	SDN	MLB	29	1.27	3.89	4.50	2.2	93.2	54.1	8.6	48.2
2018	MIL	MLB	30	1.16	3.50	4.51	1.8	92.2	48.1	9.1	48.9
2019	MIL	MLB	31	1.25	4.09	4.56	1.0	92.0	51.3	8.8	48

Jhoulys Chacin, continued

Pitch Shape vs LHH

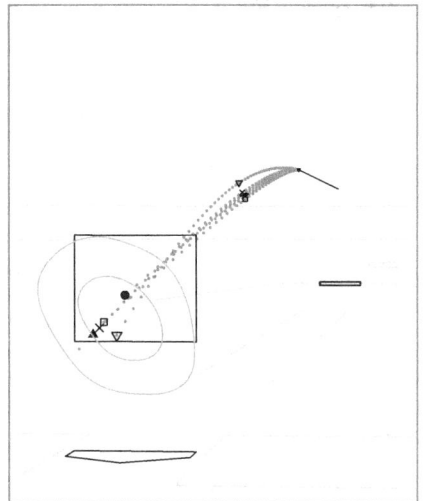

Pitch Shape vs RHH

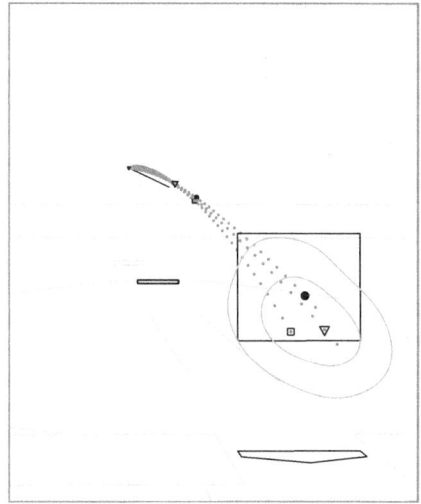

Type		Frequency	Velocity	H Movement	V Movement
●	Fastball	12.9%	90.4 [93]	-6.2 [102]	-17.8 [94]
☐	Sinker	35.2%	90.6 [90]	-13.2 [95]	-23.5 [90]
+	Cutter	0.1%	86.1 [84]	2.6 [104]	-26 [91]
▲	Changeup	2.2%	83.3 [92]	-7.9 [118]	-29.2 [95]
✕	Splitter	4.5%	86.5 [104]	-6 [108]	-28.8 [103]
▽	Slider	43.9%	79.8 [79]	12.2 [132]	-36.2 [90]
◇	Curveball	1.2%	75.8 [90]	11.7 [116]	-46.6 [103]
⊕	Slow Curveball				
✷	Knuckleball				
▼	Screwball				

Milwaukee Brewers 2019

Alex Claudio   LHP

Born: 01/31/92   Age: 27   Bats: L   Throws: L
Height: 6'3"   Weight: 180   Origin: Round 27, 2010 Draft (#826 overall)

YEAR	TEAM	LVL	AGE	W	L	SV	G	GS	IP	H	HR	BB/9	K/9	K	GB%	BABIP
2016	ROU	AAA	24	0	0	1	6	0	16^1	7	0	2.2	4.4	8	71%	.156
2016	TEX	MLB	24	4	1	0	39	0	51^2	55	2	1.7	5.9	34	63%	.312
2017	TEX	MLB	25	4	2	11	70	1	82^2	71	5	1.6	6.1	56	68%	.269
2018	TEX	MLB	26	4	2	1	66	1	68^1	91	4	1.7	5.4	41	64%	.366
2019	MIL	MLB	27	2	2	0	43	0	45	46	5	2.9	6.7	34	59%	.296

Breakout: 25%   Improve: 50%   Collapse: 23%   Attrition: 13%   MLB: 91%
Comparables: Jeremy Accardo, Bryan Shaw, Luis Avilan

Claudio was never really expected to be a big-league pitcher, so the fact that he beat out Yu Darvish, Cole Hamels and everyone else to become the Rangers' pitcher of the year in 2017 is remarkable. In 2018, however, Claudio's performance matched his scouting reports a bit more closely. Rough year notwithstanding, there are few things in life that can prompt the sort of joy as watching hitters flail and miss at Claudio's high-60s changeup.

    Here is an inclusive list; we will not be taking any more submissions: Watching guys with popped collars walk into a tree while looking at their phones. Cats chasing a laser pointer and falling into their water bowl. Drunk relatives dancing at a wedding and knocking over a whole table of cake. Martin Shkreli going to prison. When Charlie Brown tries to kick the football, but Lucy pulls it out and tricks him *yet again*. That GIF where Nick Young turns around with his arms up but the ball clangs off the rim. Watching a dude attempt to impress women with a double backflip dive but instead he does a super-loud belly-flop.

YEAR	TEAM	LVL	AGE	WHIP	ERA	DRA	WARP	MPH	FB%	WHF	CSP
2016	ROU	AAA	24	0.67	0.55	3.15	0.3				
2016	TEX	MLB	24	1.26	2.79	4.50	0.3	88.2	55.6	11	46.1
2017	TEX	MLB	25	1.04	2.50	3.77	1.3	88.0	56.6	10.6	45.8
2018	TEX	MLB	26	1.52	4.48	4.69	0.2	87.6	52	12.3	45.1
2019	MIL	MLB	27	1.33	4.04	4.44	0.2	87.4	55.1	11.6	46.1

Alex Claudio, continued

Pitch Shape vs LHH

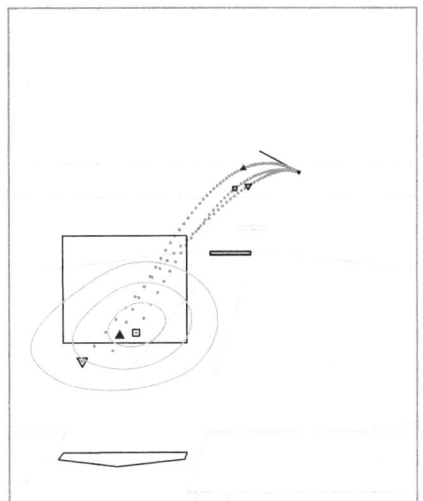

Pitch Shape vs RHH

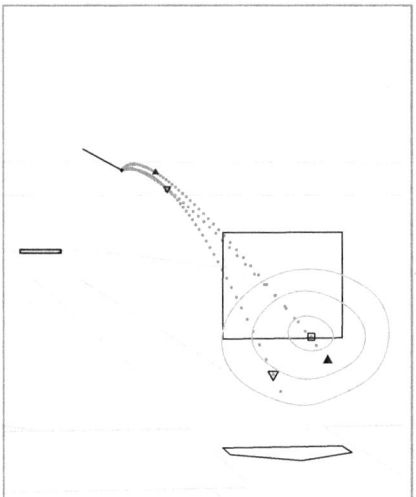

Type		Frequency	Velocity	H Movement	V Movement
●	Fastball				
☐	Sinker	52.0%	86.4 [70]	15.5 [76]	-37.2 [45]
+	Cutter				
▲	Changeup	36.5%	71.4 [45]	17.5 [67]	-50.8 [30]
×	Splitter				
▽	Slider	11.5%	76.1 [63]	-6.2 [106]	-40.9 [77]
◇	Curveball				
⊕	Slow Curveball				
✳	Knuckleball				
▼	Screwball				

Zach Davies   RHP

Born: 02/07/93   Age: 26   Bats: R   Throws: R
Height: 6'0"   Weight: 155   Origin: Round 26, 2011 Draft (#785 overall)

YEAR	TEAM	LVL	AGE	W	L	SV	G	GS	IP	H	HR	BB/9	K/9	K	GB%	BABIP
2016	CSP	AAA	23	0	0	0	2	2	9	6	0	2.0	11.0	11	44%	.261
2016	MIL	MLB	23	11	7	0	28	28	163[1]	166	20	2.1	7.4	135	47%	.302
2017	MIL	MLB	24	17	9	0	33	33	191[1]	204	20	2.6	5.8	124	51%	.302
2018	CSP	AAA	25	0	3	0	5	5	17	18	0	6.4	6.9	13	44%	.333
2018	BLX	AA	25	1	1	0	2	2	11	7	1	3.3	9.8	12	54%	.240
2018	WIS	A	25	1	0	0	4	4	19	19	2	0.0	9.0	19	63%	.347
2018	MIL	MLB	25	2	7	0	13	13	66	67	8	2.9	6.7	49	48%	.299
2019	MIL	MLB	26	8	6	0	21	21	119[2]	116	13	2.7	7.9	105	47%	.295

Breakout: 27%   Improve: 67%   Collapse: 10%   Attrition: 9%   MLB: 87%
Comparables: Kendall Graveman, Erasmo Ramirez, Joe Blanton

In the face of adversity, how does a pitcher respond? Davies lost much of the season to a series of rotator cuff and back injuries, and setbacks that necessitated lengthy rehab work in the minors. Curiously, at the MLB level Davies remained Davies, a true sinker-first pitcher who also works with variations of a cut fastball, looping curve and that gorgeous changeup. Davies basically threw his arsenal at a similar rate to his solid 2017 campaign, but he yielded more strikeouts thanks to his sinker and cutter. Despite the adversity, nothing major changed for Davies; the righty stuck with his arsenal, stuck with his general operation in the low strike zone and ticked up those whiffs at only moderate tradeoff to the ground balls. All of this is interesting because it's easy to imagine a counterfactual in which Davies is injured, the stuff backs up, the approach changes and a new pitcher emerges. Instead it seems that adversity hardly disrupted the Davies game plan.

YEAR	TEAM	LVL	AGE	WHIP	ERA	DRA	WARP	MPH	FB%	WHF	CSP
2016	CSP	AAA	23	0.89	2.00	2.14	0.3				
2016	MIL	MLB	23	1.25	3.97	3.77	3.0	91.4	56	8.9	42.8
2017	MIL	MLB	24	1.35	3.90	4.77	1.7	91.2	57.8	7.6	44.9
2018	CSP	AAA	25	1.76	6.35	4.74	0.2				
2018	BLX	AA	25	1.00	4.09	2.01	0.4				
2018	WIS	A	25	1.00	2.84	2.98	0.5				
2018	MIL	MLB	25	1.33	4.77	4.68	0.5	91.8	56.5	8.7	43.6
2019	MIL	MLB	26	1.27	3.79	4.23	1.1	91.0	57.9	8.4	44.6

Zach Davies, continued

Pitch Shape vs LHH

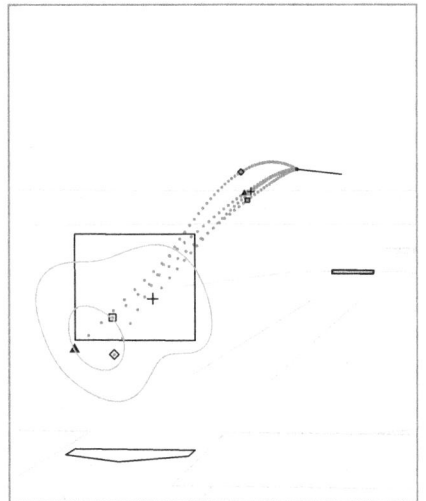

Pitch Shape vs RHH

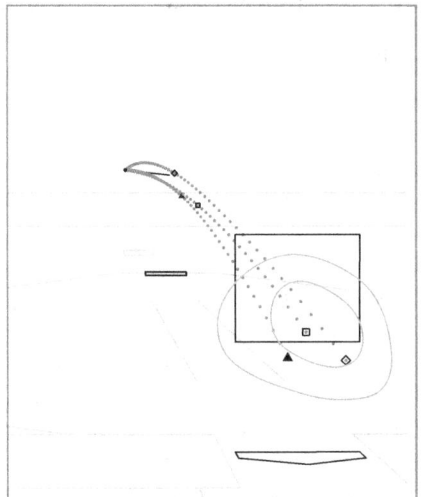

Type		Frequency	Velocity	H Movement	V Movement
●	Fastball				
☐	Sinker	56.5%	90.5 [90]	-14.4 [85]	-20.6 [99]
+	Cutter	13.1%	88.1 [96]	-0.1 [88]	-21.4 [109]
▲	Changeup	12.5%	81.1 [83]	-12.7 [92]	-30.4 [91]
×	Splitter				
▽	Slider	1.5%	82.7 [92]	5.3 [102]	-35.9 [91]
◇	Curveball	16.4%	76.1 [91]	9.6 [108]	-54.2 [86]
⊕	Slow Curveball				
✳	Knuckleball				
▼	Screwball				

Junior Guerra RHP

Born: 01/16/85   Age: 34   Bats: R   Throws: R
Height: 6'0"   Weight: 205   Origin: International Free Agent, 2001

YEAR	TEAM	LVL	AGE	W	L	SV	G	GS	IP	H	HR	BB/9	K/9	K	GB%	BABIP
2016	CSP	AAA	31	0	2	0	5	5	26²	18	2	3.7	8.4	25	40%	.235
2016	MIL	MLB	31	9	3	0	20	20	121²	94	10	3.2	7.4	100	47%	.250
2017	CSP	AAA	32	2	2	0	6	6	30	27	0	3.6	6.0	20	47%	.303
2017	MIL	MLB	32	1	4	0	21	14	70¹	61	18	5.5	8.6	67	36%	.236
2018	MIL	MLB	33	6	9	0	31	26	141	143	19	3.5	8.7	136	45%	.313
2019	MIL	MLB	34	4	3	0	56	3	71	62	9	3.7	8.9	70	43%	.280

Breakout: 15%   Improve: 32%   Collapse: 27%   Attrition: 17%   MLB: 79%
Comparables: Chris Narveson, Eric Stults, Jorge De La Rosa

In the critically acclaimed film *The Aristocats*, it goes unspoken that everybody wants to be a cat because of their penchant for extra lives. Guerra can relate, as this cat just received *at least* his fourth go-round in professional ball. From catcher to international pitcher of intrigue to waiver fodder to surging ace, now Guerra has already turned a failed rotational stint into a bullpen reinvention. In September, the Brewers employed Guerra as part of their 40-man roster pitching depth squad, and to everyone's surprise the splitter-slider master emerged as a fastball-curveball relief ace. Guerra's got the guts to close, the guile to start and the brains to reinvent himself to seize every opportunity.

YEAR	TEAM	LVL	AGE	WHIP	ERA	DRA	WARP	MPH	FB%	WHF	CSP
2016	CSP	AAA	31	1.09	4.05	3.86	0.5				
2016	MIL	MLB	31	1.13	2.81	4.19	1.6	95.5	61.6	11.6	45.5
2017	CSP	AAA	32	1.30	2.10	6.15	-0.1				
2017	MIL	MLB	32	1.48	5.12	6.31	-0.6	93.9	64.8	11.8	41.4
2018	MIL	MLB	33	1.40	4.09	4.50	1.3	95.1	69	11.6	46.5
2019	MIL	MLB	34	1.27	4.11	4.52	0.3	93.8	65.2	11.5	43.9

Junior Guerra, continued

Pitch Shape vs LHH

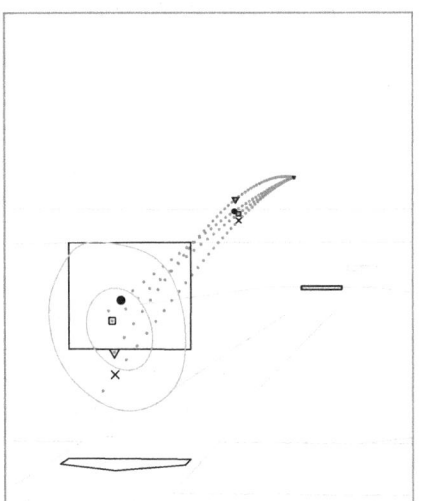

Pitch Shape vs RHH

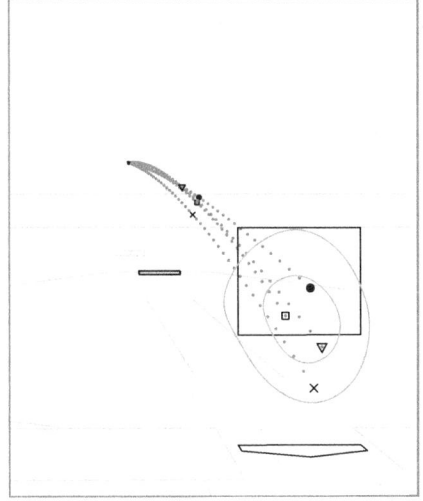

Type	Frequency	Velocity	H Movement	V Movement
● Fastball	39.0%	93.6 [104]	-4.7 [109]	-12.6 [110]
☐ Sinker	30.0%	93.9 [107]	-12.9 [98]	-17.7 [109]
+ Cutter				
▲ Changeup				
× Splitter	15.9%	87.1 [108]	-4.1 [115]	-24.5 [121]
▽ Slider	12.6%	84.4 [100]	5.1 [101]	-34.2 [97]
◇ Curveball	2.4%	82.5 [115]	5.9 [92]	-42.7 [112]
⊕ Slow Curveball				
✳ Knuckleball				
▼ Screwball				

Milwaukee Brewers 2019

Josh Hader LHP

Born: 04/07/94 Age: 25 Bats: L Throws: L
Height: 6'3" Weight: 185 Origin: Round 19, 2012 Draft (#582 overall)

YEAR	TEAM	LVL	AGE	W	L	SV	G	GS	IP	H	HR	BB/9	K/9	K	GB%	BABIP
2016	BLX	AA	22	2	1	0	11	11	57	38	1	3.0	11.5	73	41%	.291
2016	CSP	AAA	22	1	7	0	14	14	69	63	5	4.7	11.5	88	43%	.345
2017	CSP	AAA	23	3	4	0	12	12	52	49	14	5.4	8.8	51	37%	.265
2017	MIL	MLB	23	2	3	0	35	0	47²	25	4	4.2	12.8	68	36%	.233
2018	MIL	MLB	24	6	1	12	55	0	81¹	36	9	3.3	15.8	143	31%	.220
2019	MIL	MLB	25	4	3	14	64	0	67²	41	6	3.9	14.2	107	36%	.278

Breakout: 29% Improve: 57% Collapse: 20% Attrition: 15% MLB: 87%
Comparables: Carl Edwards Jr., Francisco Liriano, Kevin Siegrist

This historic, role-bending strikeout reliever whiffed on social media content and damage control. Hader's 2018 was a brilliant demonstration of how quickly the tides can change in terms of baseball strategy and pitcher usage, but it was an equally devastating demonstration of the aloof privilege afforded many white, American baseball prospects. If you missed the unearthing of Hader's past offensive tweets, the fallout was what you'd expect. Hader issued an apology meant to assuage his clubhouse moreso than people impacted by his actions, a course that was also taken by Hader's parent organization and MLB. Brewers fans gave the young flamethrower a standing ovation at their first opportunity, demonstrating their approval to sweep this thing under the rug. "Boys will be boys, everyone makes stupid mistakes." People affected by these actions don't have it so easy, often carrying burdens from continued assaults against their identities that are heightened by the mundane return to "everyday life" enjoyed by everyone else. Hader will go on compiling three-inning saves and jaw-dropping strikeout totals, and more hate speech will be unearthed from a new group of MLB youngsters; hopefully next time MLB, teams and players orient their apologies and punishments in the proper direction.

YEAR	TEAM	LVL	AGE	WHIP	ERA	DRA	WARP	MPH	FB%	WHF	CSP
2016	BLX	AA	22	1.00	0.95	2.31	1.9				
2016	CSP	AAA	22	1.43	5.22	4.55	0.6				
2017	CSP	AAA	23	1.54	5.37	5.19	0.3				
2017	MIL	MLB	23	0.99	2.08	3.31	1.0	96.8	81.4	18.4	49.4
2018	MIL	MLB	24	0.81	2.43	2.00	2.7	96.9	79.1	20.5	51.7
2019	MIL	MLB	25	1.02	2.20	2.75	1.6	96.6	81.7	20.3	51.9

Josh Hader, continued

Pitch Shape vs LHH

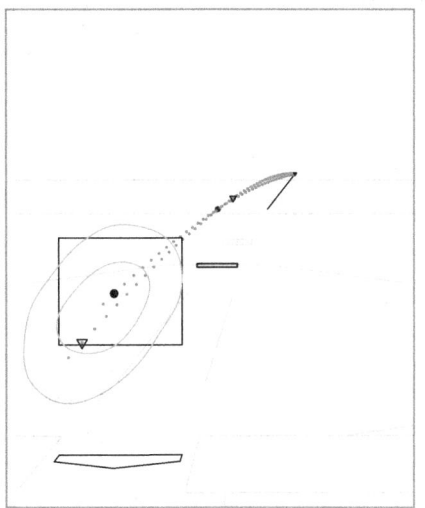

Pitch Shape vs RHH

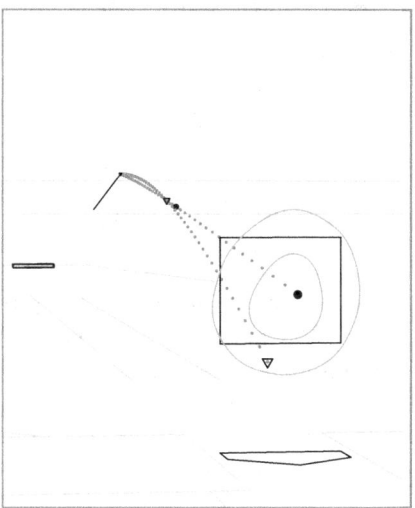

Type		Frequency	Velocity	H Movement	V Movement
●	Fastball	79.1%	95.2 [108]	8.8 [90]	-11.9 [112]
☐	Sinker				
+	Cutter				
▲	Changeup	0.3%	87.1 [107]	12.7 [92]	-26.9 [101]
✕	Splitter				
▽	Slider	20.6%	82.5 [91]	-4.4 [98]	-32 [103]
◇	Curveball				
⊕	Slow Curveball				
✻	Knuckleball				
▼	Screwball				

Adrian Houser RHP

Born: 02/02/93 Age: 26 Bats: R Throws: R
Height: 6'4" Weight: 235 Origin: Round 2, 2011 Draft (#69 overall)

YEAR	TEAM	LVL	AGE	W	L	SV	G	GS	IP	H	HR	BB/9	K/9	K	GB%	BABIP
2016	BLX	AA	23	3	7	0	13	13	70^1	76	5	2.8	7.2	56	62%	.326
2017	WIS	A	24	1	0	0	3	2	9	5	0	0.0	11.0	11	71%	.238
2018	BLX	AA	25	0	1	0	8	8	26^2	30	3	2.4	10.1	30	51%	.365
2018	MIL	MLB	25	0	0	0	7	0	13^2	13	0	4.6	5.3	8	40%	.302
2018	CSP	AAA	25	2	3	0	13	13	52	66	6	3.1	6.4	37	54%	.357
2019	MIL	MLB	26	3	3	0	32	5	51^2	53	8	3.6	8.0	46	52%	.299

Breakout: 9% Improve: 22% Collapse: 9% Attrition: 20% MLB: 39%
Comparables: Stephen Fife, Gus Schlosser, Chris Stratton

For the Overall Future Potential files, the organizational depth role can be grueling. Milwaukee ran a real, live shuttle crew in 2018, and first recalled Houser from Double-A on April 6. On April 8, Houser allowed one hit and struck out three in two innings of work against the Cubs, averaging around 95 mph and showcasing both his change and curve. The big righty was promptly optioned back to Double-A, where he began a stretch of eight starts. May 26 was Houser's next recall, this time with two scoreless innings against the Mets also adorned with three strikeouts. The Brewers almost immediately optioned Houser to Triple-A, which is kind of a promotion in this context. On June 17, he was recalled again, and this time stayed for nearly two weeks before his Triple-A demotion. The Brewers used one-day recalls on July 12 and August 11; on July 12, the results weren't as good, but they were great in August. That's approximately 20 days of MLB service on a prorated 40-man roster contract, including at least 11 moves in six months, for a big fastball, big frame, high-floor MLB pitcher.

YEAR	TEAM	LVL	AGE	WHIP	ERA	DRA	WARP	MPH	FB%	WHF	CSP
2016	BLX	AA	23	1.39	5.25	4.75	0.3				
2017	WIS	A	24	0.56	1.00	4.05	0.1				
2018	BLX	AA	25	1.39	4.72	4.45	0.3				
2018	MIL	MLB	25	1.46	3.29	5.04	0.0	96.1	66.4	11.1	44.7
2018	CSP	AAA	25	1.62	5.19	4.56	0.6				
2019	MIL	MLB	26	1.42	4.72	5.06	-0.1	95.7	67.6	11.3	45.5

Adrian Houser, continued

Pitch Shape vs LHH

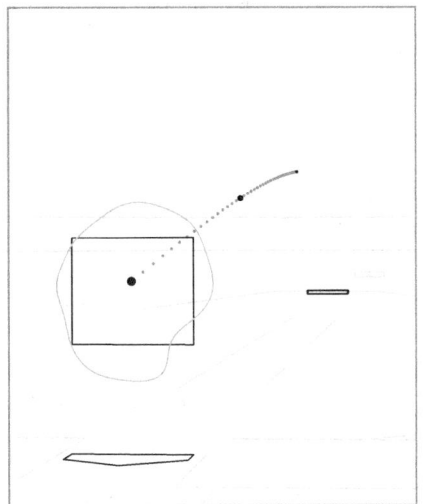

Pitch Shape vs RHH

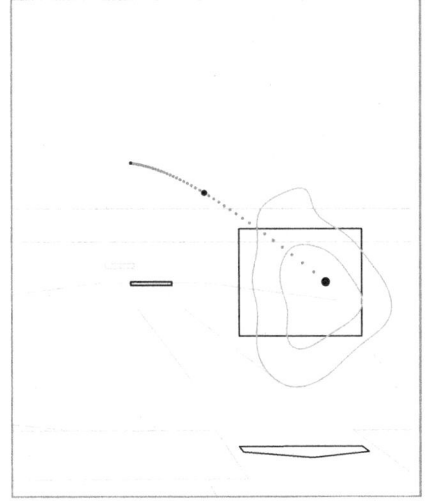

Type	Frequency	Velocity	H Movement	V Movement
● Fastball	61.1%	94.8 [107]	-3.7 [114]	-14 [106]
□ Sinker	5.3%	94.5 [110]	-13.6 [92]	-18.6 [106]
+ Cutter				
▲ Changeup	14.2%	85.2 [99]	-11.6 [98]	-29.7 [93]
× Splitter				
▽ Slider				
◇ Curveball	19.5%	81.3 [110]	5 [88]	-48.5 [99]
✜ Slow Curveball				
✱ Knuckleball				
▼ Screwball				

Milwaukee Brewers 2019

Jeremy Jeffress   RHP
Born: 09/21/87   Age: 31   Bats: R   Throws: R
Height: 6'0"   Weight: 205   Origin: Round 1, 2006 Draft (#16 overall)

YEAR	TEAM	LVL	AGE	W	L	SV	G	GS	IP	H	HR	BB/9	K/9	K	GB%	BABIP
2016	MIL	MLB	28	2	2	27	47	0	44^2	45	2	2.2	7.1	35	59%	.312
2016	TEX	MLB	28	1	0	0	12	0	13^1	10	0	4.7	4.7	7	70%	.270
2017	TEX	MLB	29	1	2	0	39	0	40^2	49	8	4.2	6.4	29	56%	.328
2017	MIL	MLB	29	4	0	0	22	1	24^2	24	2	5.5	8.0	22	65%	.301
2018	MIL	MLB	30	8	1	15	73	0	76^2	49	5	3.2	10.4	89	58%	.249
2019	MIL	MLB	31	3	3	8	59	0	62	53	6	3.8	9.7	67	55%	.296

Breakout: 25%   Improve: 46%   Collapse: 25%   Attrition: 12%   MLB: 90%
Comparables: Peter Moylan, Chad Bradford, Pedro Feliciano

Redemption is a difficult storyline because if you lean too hard on the moral, you'll miss the process. Jeffress' redemption is manifold, and his third go-round in Milwaukee demonstrated that some players just *belong* in some organizations. Player development takes a village, from the player to the front office and support staff. Jeffress is undoubtedly a success of the human side of the game. But don't let these morals write the full story. The high-leverage chameleon will work in any inning, splitting a plurality of appearances from the sixth through the ninth in 2018. He'll enter in tricky inherited runner situations. And, 55 percent of the time, he entered when the game was within one run. Stomping and huffing on the mound, glaring past the batter to get the sign, Jeffress became a curveball-first pitcher while also balancing usage between his electric sinker and traditional hard-riding fastball. This tweak helped multiply strikeouts without sacrificing excellent ground-ball abilities. Here the process was as important as the moral, which helps to explain why Jeffress' redemption placed him near the top of NL relief ranks, well beyond his previous profile as just another potential high-leverage reliever.

YEAR	TEAM	LVL	AGE	WHIP	ERA	DRA	WARP	MPH	FB%	WHF	CSP
2016	MIL	MLB	28	1.25	2.22	4.45	0.3	98.3	73.7	11.2	50.3
2016	TEX	MLB	28	1.27	2.70	5.49	-0.1	96.9	83.3	7.8	49
2017	TEX	MLB	29	1.67	5.31	6.45	-0.6	96.4	67.9	10.2	46.2
2017	MIL	MLB	29	1.58	3.65	4.42	0.2	96.7	62	11.7	42.2
2018	MIL	MLB	30	0.99	1.29	2.62	2.0	97.3	53.2	14.7	47.6
2019	MIL	MLB	31	1.27	3.27	3.81	0.7	96.3	61.5	12.5	46.9

Jeremy Jeffress, continued

Pitch Shape vs LHH

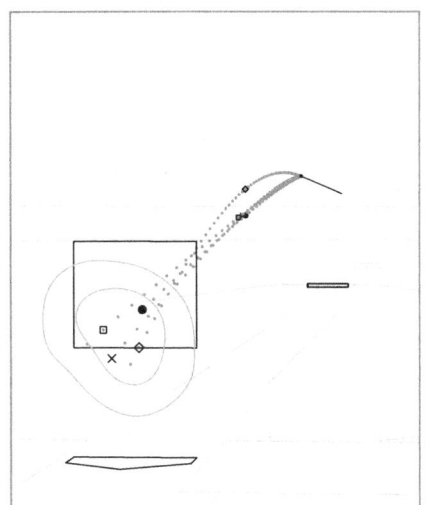

Pitch Shape vs RHH

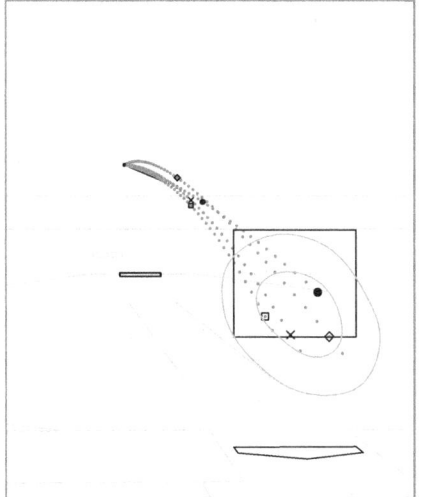

Type	Frequency	Velocity	H Movement	V Movement
● Fastball	24.9%	96.2 [112]	-5.4 [106]	-12.7 [110]
□ Sinker	28.2%	95.7 [116]	-14.8 [82]	-19.6 [102]
+ Cutter				
▲ Changeup	0.2%	91.4 [124]	-11.5 [99]	-27.5 [99]
✕ Splitter	15.8%	91.2 [130]	-9.3 [96]	-27.3 [109]
▽ Slider				
◇ Curveball	30.8%	81.7 [112]	9.2 [106]	-43.9 [109]
⊕ Slow Curveball				
✱ Knuckleball				
▼ Screwball				

Corey Knebel RHP

Born: 11/26/91 Age: 27 Bats: R Throws: R
Height: 6'4" Weight: 220 Origin: Round 1, 2013 Draft (#39 overall)

YEAR	TEAM	LVL	AGE	W	L	SV	G	GS	IP	H	HR	BB/9	K/9	K	GB%	BABIP
2016	CSP	AAA	24	1	0	2	11	2	13^2	5	0	2.0	9.2	14	66%	.172
2016	MIL	MLB	24	1	4	2	35	0	32^2	32	3	4.4	10.5	38	43%	.333
2017	MIL	MLB	25	1	4	39	76	0	76	48	6	4.7	14.9	126	39%	.311
2018	MIL	MLB	26	4	3	16	57	0	55^1	38	7	3.6	14.3	88	50%	.304
2019	MIL	MLB	27	3	2	18	59	0	62	44	5	4.1	12.6	87	45%	.294

Breakout: 33% Improve: 56% Collapse: 27% Attrition: 14% MLB: 97%
Comparables: Cody Allen, Ken Giles, Jordan Walden

It would be hard to believe a serious account of the 2018 season in which the Brewers won 96 games and Knebel might have been the fourth-best reliever on the staff. Yet Knebel battled injuries, command concerns and general ineffectiveness throughout much of the season. His overall stuff remained largely intact, with a hard fastball-curveball duo for the ex-closer. Refined command and mechanics means Knebel can throw the curve more than 35 percent of the time, however, and when that approach works, you can put the capital-"K" back in Knebel. He had a 5.01 ERA on September 1, but then tossed 16 1/3 scoreless innings with a 33/3 K/BB ratio in the final month and reclaimed a prominent role in the playoffs.

YEAR	TEAM	LVL	AGE	WHIP	ERA	DRA	WARP	MPH	FB%	WHF	CSP
2016	CSP	AAA	24	0.59	1.32	3.26	0.3				
2016	MIL	MLB	24	1.47	4.68	5.45	-0.2	97.7	72.3	9.3	48
2017	MIL	MLB	25	1.16	1.78	3.09	1.8	98.9	71.8	15.4	47.4
2018	MIL	MLB	26	1.08	3.58	2.53	1.5	98.4	70.9	14.5	49.2
2019	MIL	MLB	27	1.16	2.45	3.01	1.3	98.0	72.4	14.3	48.9

Corey Knebel, continued

Pitch Shape vs LHH

Pitch Shape vs RHH

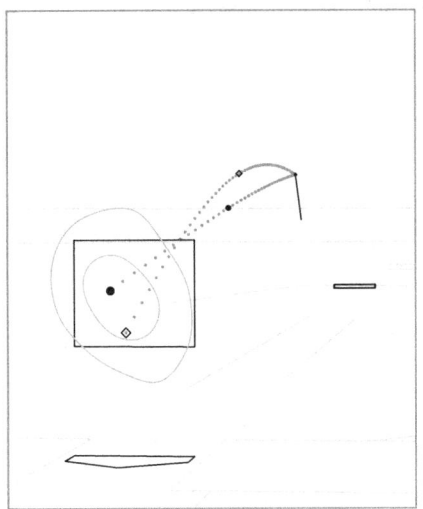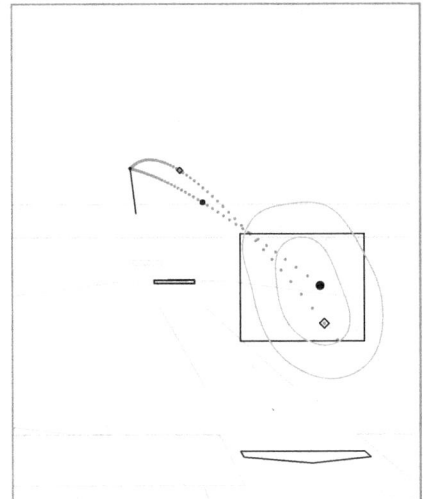

Type	Frequency	Velocity	H Movement	V Movement
● Fastball	70.9%	97.4 [116]	-2.6 [119]	-11.1 [115]
☐ Sinker				
+ Cutter				
▲ Changeup				
✕ Splitter				
▽ Slider				
◇ Curveball	29.1%	82 [113]	9.4 [107]	-51 [93]
⊕ Slow Curveball				
✳ Knuckleball				
▼ Screwball				

Freddy Peralta RHP

Born: 06/04/96 Age: 23 Bats: R Throws: R
Height: 5'11" Weight: 175 Origin: International Free Agent, 2013

YEAR	TEAM	LVL	AGE	W	L	SV	G	GS	IP	H	HR	BB/9	K/9	K	GB%	BABIP
2016	WIS	A	20	4	1	2	16	8	60	45	3	3.6	11.6	77	35%	.292
2016	BRV	A+	20	0	3	0	8	2	22	27	4	4.9	8.2	20	51%	.365
2017	CAR	A+	21	1	3	0	12	8	56^1	39	6	5.0	12.5	78	39%	.268
2017	BLX	AA	21	2	5	1	13	11	63^2	38	2	4.4	12.9	91	44%	.267
2018	CSP	AAA	22	6	2	0	13	13	61	49	1	4.1	12.8	87	48%	.343
2018	MIL	MLB	22	6	4	0	16	14	78^1	49	8	4.6	11.0	96	33%	.237
2019	MIL	MLB	23	5	4	0	15	15	79	63	10	4.2	11.5	102	38%	.290

Breakout: 18% Improve: 41% Collapse: 17% Attrition: 21% MLB: 68%
Comparables: Alex Reyes, Zach Braddock, Rubby De La Rosa

What makes Peralta's fastball special is that he throws several variations in one pitch, taking a little bit off when necessary, bending it like a cutter or trying to run it when he needs a different look. By the NLCS, Peralta was demonstrating increased velocity out of the bullpen while maintaining the velocity and movement variations that make the pitch tick. The easy money is on Peralta staying in a supporting role, but the lesson of 2018 should be loudly learned: the lack of a certain role and the existence of clear shortcomings will not stop Peralta from making an impact.

YEAR	TEAM	LVL	AGE	WHIP	ERA	DRA	WARP	MPH	FB%	WHF	CSP
2016	WIS	A	20	1.15	2.85	3.06	1.3				
2016	BRV	A+	20	1.77	5.73	3.88	0.3				
2017	CAR	A+	21	1.24	3.04	3.55	1.1				
2017	BLX	AA	21	1.08	2.26	2.68	1.9				
2018	CSP	AAA	22	1.26	3.10	2.96	1.8				
2018	MIL	MLB	22	1.14	4.25	5.21	0.1	93.8	77.6	12	49.2
2019	MIL	MLB	23	1.24	3.59	4.04	0.9	93.7	80.4	12.5	51

Freddy Peralta, continued

Pitch Shape vs LHH

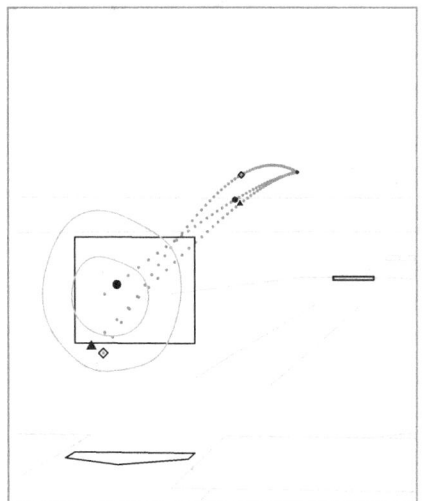

Pitch Shape vs RHH

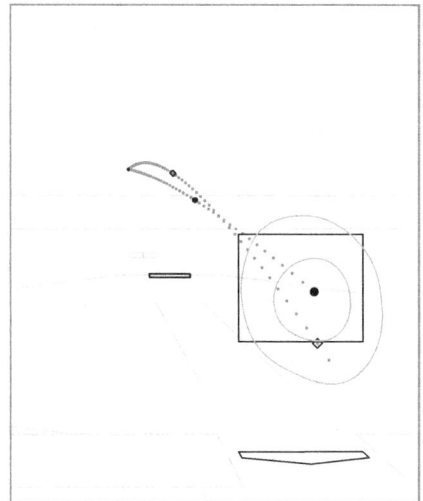

Type	Frequency	Velocity	H Movement	V Movement
● Fastball	77.6%	91.4 [96]	-2.6 [119]	-13.7 [107]
☐ Sinker				
+ Cutter				
▲ Changeup	2.8%	86.9 [106]	-8.1 [117]	-24 [110]
✕ Splitter				
▽ Slider				
◇ Curveball	19.6%	77 [95]	6.6 [95]	-50.4 [95]
⊕ Slow Curveball				
✶ Knuckleball				
▼ Screwball				

Milwaukee Brewers 2019

Jake Petricka   RHP
Born: 06/05/88   Age: 31   Bats: R   Throws: R
Height: 6'5"   Weight: 220   Origin: Round 2, 2010 Draft (#63 overall)

YEAR	TEAM	LVL	AGE	W	L	SV	G	GS	IP	H	HR	BB/9	K/9	K	GB%	BABIP
2016	CHA	MLB	28	0	0	0	9	0	8	8	1	9.0	7.9	7	71%	.304
2017	CHA	MLB	29	1	1	0	27	0	25²	39	6	2.1	9.1	26	48%	.398
2018	BUF	AAA	30	0	0	2	16	0	23	20	1	2.0	5.5	14	79%	.284
2018	TOR	MLB	30	3	1	0	41	0	45²	59	6	3.2	8.1	41	53%	.379
2019	MIL	MLB	31	1	1	0	27	0	28	28	4	4.3	8.0	25	53%	.303

Breakout: 31%   Improve: 40%   Collapse: 17%   Attrition: 14%   MLB: 76%
Comparables: Rafael Perez, Ryan Webb, Bobby Parnell

Like any well-intentioned but ill-fated cartoon character, Petricka careened down a path that was littered with warning signs at every turn. "Turn back: labral tear ahead!" "Watch out—nerve transposition!" "Beware of flexor tendon debridement!" While he hasn't gone over the metaphorical cliff of career-killing injury or total irrelevancy just yet, the hard-throwing reliever's upside—a nasty sinker and a slider that, on its good days, induced a .235 average and 21 percent whiff rate—has been buried by dynamite explosion after dynamite explosion. If he makes any impact in pro ball during 2019, it'll likely be as organizational depth.

YEAR	TEAM	LVL	AGE	WHIP	ERA	DRA	WARP	MPH	FB%	WHF	CSP
2016	CHA	MLB	28	2.00	4.50	6.19	-0.1	97.4	75	9.6	44.2
2017	CHA	MLB	29	1.75	7.01	6.59	-0.4	97.0	70.2	8.4	49.8
2018	BUF	AAA	30	1.09	0.78	3.57	0.4				
2018	TOR	MLB	30	1.64	4.53	5.66	-0.4	97.5	65.8	12.2	45.8
2019	MIL	MLB	31	1.50	4.78	5.02	-0.1	96.5	67.4	10.8	46.5

Jake Petricka, continued

Pitch Shape vs LHH

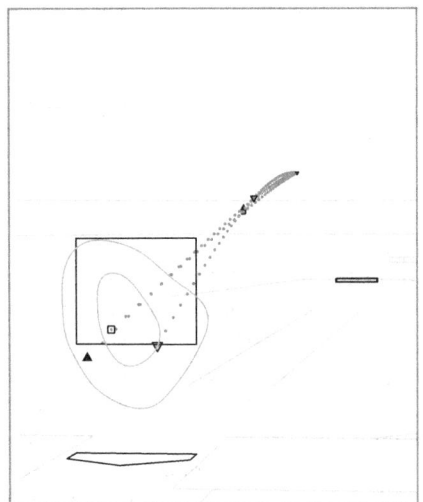

Pitch Shape vs RHH

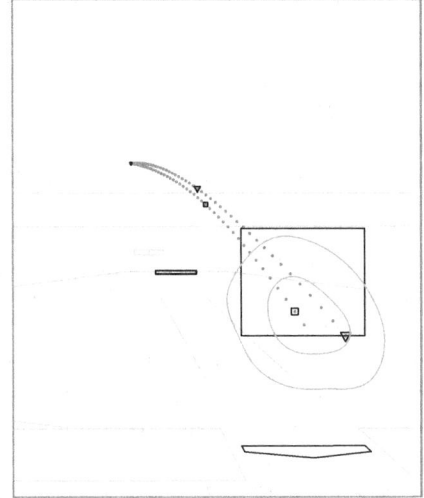

Type	Frequency	Velocity	H Movement	V Movement
● Fastball	1.4%	95.7 [110]	-11 [80]	-14.6 [103]
□ Sinker	64.4%	95.4 [115]	-14.4 [85]	-18.1 [107]
+ Cutter				
▲ Changeup	8.4%	89.1 [115]	-15.6 [77]	-26.3 [103]
× Splitter				
▽ Slider	25.8%	86.2 [108]	0 [79]	-31.4 [105]
◇ Curveball				
⊕ Slow Curveball				
✱ Knuckleball				
▼ Screwball				

Burch Smith RHP

Born: 04/12/90 Age: 29 Bats: R Throws: R
Height: 6'4" Weight: 225 Origin: Round 14, 2011 Draft (#443 overall)

YEAR	TEAM	LVL	AGE	W	L	SV	G	GS	IP	H	HR	BB/9	K/9	K	GB%	BABIP
2017	PCH	A+	27	3	1	0	9	8	37	26	1	4.9	8.0	33	35%	.255
2017	DUR	AAA	27	2	1	0	3	3	16^1	9	2	2.2	10.5	19	46%	.200
2018	KCA	MLB	28	1	6	0	38	6	78	90	15	4.6	8.9	77	41%	.338
2019	MIL	MLB	29	4	3	0	37	9	68^1	62	10	4.2	9.1	69	40%	.299

Breakout: 23% Improve: 39% Collapse: 15% Attrition: 15% MLB: 65%
Comparables: Jeff Samardzija, Jason Bergmann, Matt Kinney

The accepted custom for the Comeback Player of the Year is that a candidate has to have fallen from great heights and returned to at least moderate success; it's never given to someone who wasn't an All-Star, much less to an anonymous swingman-type. But with his spondaic, arboreal name straight out of a Robert Frost poem, Smith doggedly labored his way back from an early 2014 injury that led to Tommy John surgery and the associated rehab, with a four-year lacuna in his major-league stat line. There was no fanfare for a return to a season that saw far too many walks and homers, but they were major-league walks and homers, at least. Pitchers who miss that much time almost never make it within a stone's throw of the majors; Smith, to his credit, has indeed taken the road less travelled. Whether it makes a difference to the Royals, or any team, is a verse yet unwritten.

YEAR	TEAM	LVL	AGE	WHIP	ERA	DRA	WARP	MPH	FB%	WHF	CSP
2017	PCH	A+	27	1.24	2.43	5.84	-0.3				
2017	DUR	AAA	27	0.80	1.65	1.95	0.7				
2018	KCA	MLB	28	1.67	6.92	6.28	-1.1	96.1	61.8	11.1	48.9
2019	MIL	MLB	29	1.38	4.60	5.29	-0.2	95.4	61.8	11.1	48.9

Burch Smith, continued

Pitch Shape vs LHH

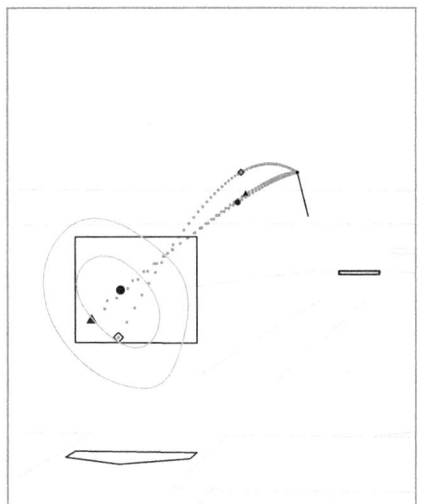

Pitch Shape vs RHH

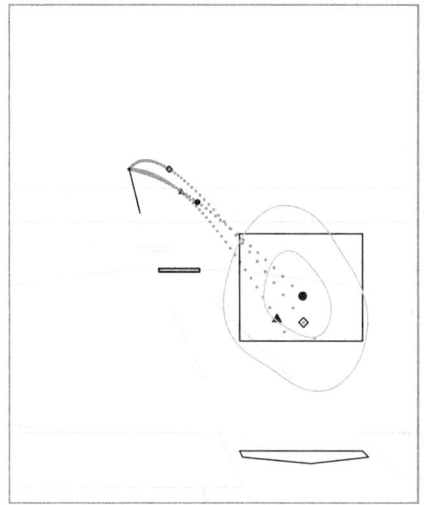

Type	Frequency	Velocity	H Movement	V Movement
● Fastball	60.9%	93.7 [104]	-5.7 [104]	-14.7 [103]
□ Sinker	0.9%	90.3 [89]	-10.7 [115]	-24.2 [87]
+ Cutter				
▲ Changeup	16.7%	82.1 [87]	-9.9 [108]	-24.5 [108]
× Splitter				
▽ Slider				
◇ Curveball	21.5%	78.4 [100]	10.8 [113]	-50.5 [95]
⊕ Slow Curveball				
✳ Knuckleball				
▼ Screwball				

Milwaukee Brewers 2019

Brent Suter   LHP

Born: 08/29/89   Age: 29   Bats: L   Throws: L
Height: 6'5"   Weight: 195   Origin: Round 31, 2012 Draft (#965 overall)

YEAR	TEAM	LVL	AGE	W	L	SV	G	GS	IP	H	HR	BB/9	K/9	K	GB%	BABIP
2016	CSP	AAA	26	6	6	2	26	15	110²	129	5	1.1	6.1	75	41%	.348
2016	MIL	MLB	26	2	2	0	14	2	21²	25	3	2.1	6.2	15	44%	.328
2017	CSP	AAA	27	3	1	0	10	8	36²	42	5	2.0	9.3	38	46%	.359
2017	MIL	MLB	27	3	2	0	22	14	81²	83	8	2.4	7.1	64	46%	.306
2018	MIL	MLB	28	8	7	0	20	18	101¹	102	18	1.7	7.5	84	36%	.281
2019	MIL	MLB	29	1	0	0	11	0	11¹	11	2	2.6	8.5	11	40%	.292

Breakout: 25%   Improve: 35%   Collapse: 16%   Attrition: 17%   MLB: 62%
Comparables: Pat Misch, Chris Rusin, J.D. Martin

Don't let those velocity vultures tell you that hard-throwers have exclusive license to the Tommy John surgery! Suter's raptor delivery pumped up above 87 mph in 2018, even averaging 88 or better during some months. Be it the southpaw's herky-jerky mechanics, rapid-fire pace, the slider usage or the increased curveball, Suter succumbed to elbow surgery in August. Even without the ability to pitch, the Environmental Science and Public Policy graduate kept bringing his Eco Meal Kit to the park, emerging as a grade-80 hype man for the contending Brewers and one of the leaders of a raucous dugout celebration crew. Suter remains one to watch in 2019, both for his potential injury recovery and re-emergence as one of the fastest-working slow-throwers in MLB, and for his earnest, joyful support for the game.

YEAR	TEAM	LVL	AGE	WHIP	ERA	DRA	WARP	MPH	FB%	WHF	CSP
2016	CSP	AAA	26	1.29	3.50	5.47	-0.3				
2016	MIL	MLB	26	1.38	3.32	6.45	-0.3	86.9	68.3	10.1	48.5
2017	CSP	AAA	27	1.36	4.42	3.79	0.8				
2017	MIL	MLB	27	1.29	3.42	4.72	0.7	88.2	70.6	10.3	49
2018	MIL	MLB	28	1.19	4.44	5.01	0.3	88.6	68.9	11.1	50.1
2019	MIL	MLB	29	1.22	4.07	4.48	0.0	87.7	69.5	10.7	49.3

Brent Suter, continued

Pitch Shape vs LHH	Pitch Shape vs RHH
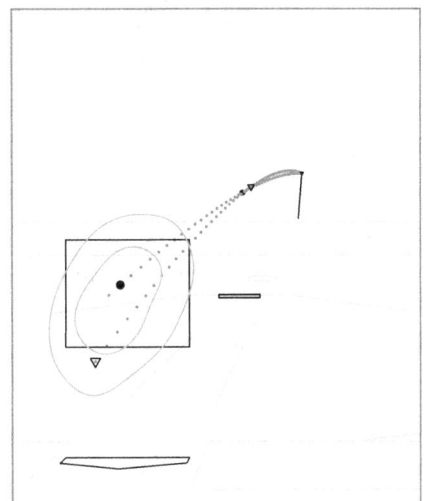	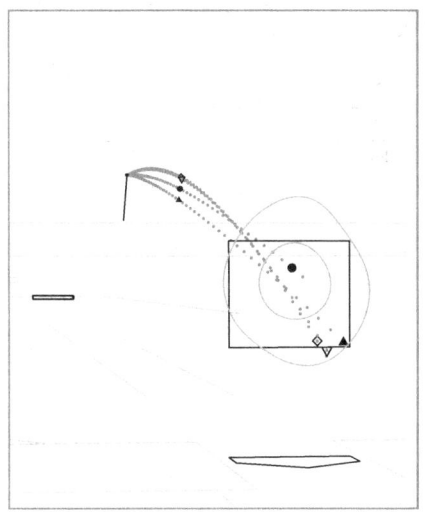

Type	Frequency	Velocity	H Movement	V Movement
● Fastball	67.9%	87.3 [83]	0.7 [127]	-19 [90]
☐ Sinker	1.0%	87.1 [73]	11.3 [111]	-21.7 [96]
+ Cutter				
▲ Changeup	12.9%	80.8 [82]	11.3 [100]	-25.7 [105]
✕ Splitter				
▽ Slider	14.8%	76.4 [64]	-5.4 [103]	-44.6 [66]
◇ Curveball	3.4%	73.8 [83]	-6.9 [96]	-49.8 [96]
✥ Slow Curveball				
✱ Knuckleball				
▼ Screwball				

Milwaukee Brewers 2019

Josh Tomlin   RHP

Born: 10/19/84   Age: 34   Bats: R   Throws: R
Height: 6'1"   Weight: 190   Origin: Round 19, 2006 Draft (#581 overall)

YEAR	TEAM	LVL	AGE	W	L	SV	G	GS	IP	H	HR	BB/9	K/9	K	GB%	BABIP
2016	CLE	MLB	31	13	9	0	30	29	174	187	36	1.0	6.1	118	44%	.276
2017	CLE	MLB	32	10	9	0	26	26	141	166	23	0.9	7.0	109	42%	.329
2018	CLE	MLB	33	2	5	0	32	9	70¹	92	25	1.5	5.9	46	32%	.286
2019	MIL	MLB	34	5	6	0	16	16	88¹	89	18	2.1	7.1	70	39%	.285

Breakout: 18%   Improve: 38%   Collapse: 15%   Attrition: 8%   MLB: 77%
Comparables: Robin Roberts, Dan Haren, Fergie Jenkins

Tomlin has always avoided walks to an almost hilarious degree. The approach has, of course, left him more susceptible to hard contact, as well as the more-than-occasional dinger, as evidenced by the fact that he's allowed more home runs than walks in every season since 2014. The problem in 2018 was that while his approach remained, he stopped missing bats almost entirely. He made seven starts from the beginning of the season through mid-May, when he was jettisoned from the rotation after allowing almost as many home runs (15) as he had strikeouts (18) in just 31 innings. He spent the rest of the year as a mop-up guy.

YEAR	TEAM	LVL	AGE	WHIP	ERA	DRA	WARP	MPH	FB%	WHF	CSP
2016	CLE	MLB	31	1.19	4.40	4.57	1.6	89.9	77.8	8.1	47.4
2017	CLE	MLB	32	1.28	4.98	4.44	1.8	89.1	71.8	9.6	49.1
2018	CLE	MLB	33	1.48	6.14	6.87	-1.4	89.6	72.7	9.4	49.9
2019	MIL	MLB	34	1.24	5.02	5.77	-0.5	88.4	73.1	8.9	48.3

Josh Tomlin, continued

Pitch Shape vs LHH

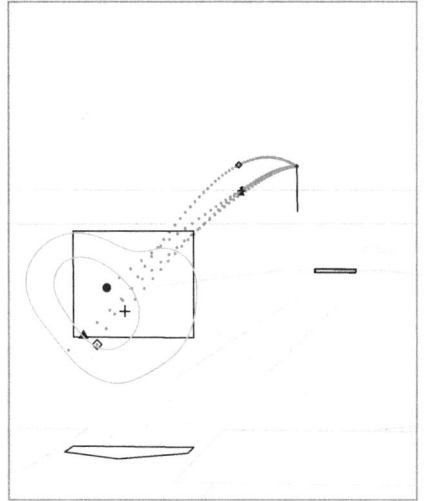

Pitch Shape vs RHH

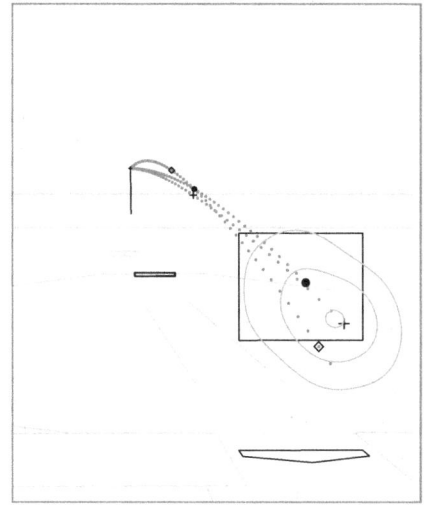

Type	Frequency	Velocity	H Movement	V Movement
● Fastball	33.6%	88.3 [86]	-8.9 [90]	-17.9 [93]
□ Sinker	0.2%	85.8 [67]	-16.3 [69]	-24.3 [87]
+ Cutter	38.9%	86.3 [85]	2.9 [106]	-23 [103]
▲ Changeup	4.5%	83.7 [93]	-12.6 [93]	-28 [98]
× Splitter				
▽ Slider				
◇ Curveball	22.8%	75.5 [89]	9.2 [106]	-53.4 [88]
⊕ Slow Curveball				
✳ Knuckleball				
▼ Screwball				

Milwaukee Brewers 2019

Brandon Woodruff RHP

Born: 02/10/93   Age: 26   Bats: L   Throws: R
Height: 6'4"   Weight: 215   Origin: Round 11, 2014 Draft (#326 overall)

YEAR	TEAM	LVL	AGE	W	L	SV	G	GS	IP	H	HR	BB/9	K/9	K	GB%	BABIP
2016	BRV	A+	23	4	1	0	8	8	44^1	33	2	2.0	9.9	49	52%	.277
2016	BLX	AA	23	10	8	0	20	20	113^2	88	4	2.4	9.8	124	49%	.286
2017	CSP	AAA	24	6	5	0	16	16	75^1	78	8	3.0	8.4	70	49%	.323
2017	MIL	MLB	24	2	3	0	8	8	43	43	5	2.9	6.7	32	50%	.292
2018	CSP	AAA	25	3	2	0	17	17	71^1	67	8	4.0	8.6	68	50%	.296
2018	MIL	MLB	25	3	0	1	19	4	42^1	36	4	3.0	10.0	47	54%	.294
2019	MIL	MLB	26	9	7	0	35	24	138	120	15	3.1	9.2	142	47%	.287

Breakout: 20%   Improve: 34%   Collapse: 24%   Attrition: 25%   MLB: 77%
Comparables: Alfredo Aceves, David Phelps, Chris Devenski

In another age, the Brewers would have simply plugged Woodruff into the rotation and allowed the big righty an opportunity to show mid-rotation potential, or at least eat innings. Only in 2018, Woodruff was not that, instead serving as a bizarre swingman between Triple-A and MLB, culminating in only four starts at the highest level. That development plan proved worthwhile as Woodruff emerged as an even harder-throwing, multi-inning arm out of the bullpen, with a new sinking fastball to run in on right-handed batters and a slower curve, too. This is the Woodruff who worked a pristine September, striking out 16 of 50 batters faced and yielding 18 ground balls against 12 fly outs. All of this makes Woodruff something of a chameleon, a flexible workhorse well-suited for an era of openers and longer relief.

YEAR	TEAM	LVL	AGE	WHIP	ERA	DRA	WARP	MPH	FB%	WHF	CSP
2016	BRV	A+	23	0.97	1.83	2.11	1.7				
2016	BLX	AA	23	1.04	3.01	2.29	3.8				
2017	CSP	AAA	24	1.37	4.30	4.01	1.4				
2017	MIL	MLB	24	1.33	4.81	5.65	0.0	96.3	60.5	9.8	46.2
2018	CSP	AAA	25	1.39	4.04	4.48	0.9				
2018	MIL	MLB	25	1.18	3.61	3.16	0.9	97.5	64.1	11.3	50.1
2019	MIL	MLB	26	1.20	3.51	3.96	1.7	96.6	63.6	10.8	49.2

Brandon Woodruff, continued

Pitch Shape vs LHH

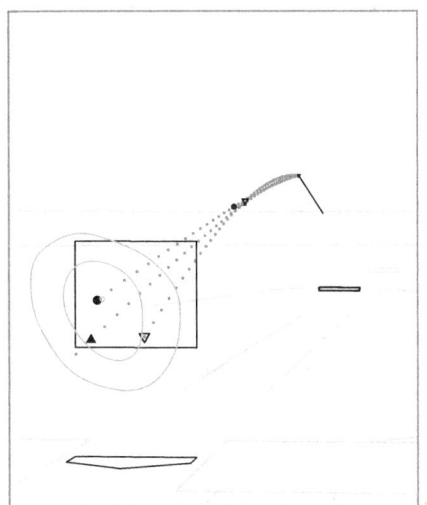

Pitch Shape vs RHH

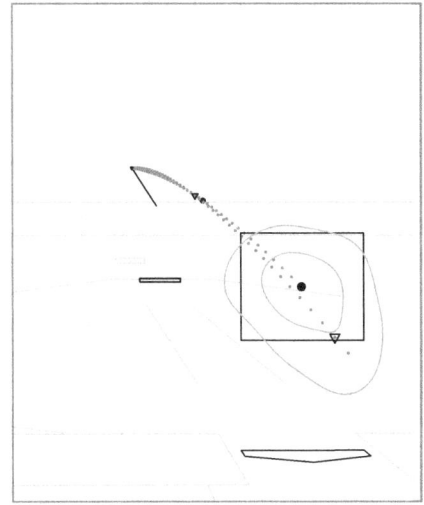

Type	Frequency	Velocity	H Movement	V Movement
● Fastball	63.1%	95.8 [111]	-8.1 [93]	-14.3 [105]
☐ Sinker	0.9%	95.9 [117]	-13.1 [96]	-17.2 [110]
+ Cutter				
▲ Changeup	11.3%	85.2 [99]	-12.9 [91]	-27.4 [100]
× Splitter				
▽ Slider	23.5%	87.4 [113]	3.4 [94]	-31.2 [105]
◇ Curveball	1.2%	78.9 [101]	3.1 [80]	-39.5 [119]
✥ Slow Curveball				
✳ Knuckleball				
▼ Screwball				

Mauricio Dubon SS

Born: 07/19/94 Age: 24 Bats: R Throws: R
Height: 6'0" Weight: 160 Origin: Round 26, 2013 Draft (#773 overall)

YEAR	TEAM	LVL	AGE	PA	R	2B	3B	HR	RBI	BB	K	SB	CS	AVG/OBP/SLG
2016	SLM	A+	21	279	53	11	3	0	29	33	25	24	4	.306/.387/.379
2016	PME	AA	21	270	48	20	6	6	40	11	36	6	3	.339/.371/.538
2017	BLX	AA	22	304	34	14	0	2	24	25	42	31	9	.276/.338/.351
2017	CSP	AAA	22	244	40	15	0	6	33	14	34	7	6	.272/.320/.420
2018	CSP	AAA	23	114	18	9	2	4	18	2	19	6	3	.343/.348/.574
2019	MIL	MLB	24	64	8	3	0	2	7	2	12	2	1	.250/.274/.400

Breakout: 19%   Improve: 37%   Collapse: 2%   Attrition: 31%   MLB: 54%
Comparables: Eduardo Nunez, Kevin Newman, Trevor Plouffe

Just when the Brewers needed a boost in the middle infield, this glove-first, high-floor shortstop tore his ACL and was finished until spring 2019. Rumor had it that Dubon was on the front office's radar at the time of the injury, which suggests that questions about the bat, or questions about his ultimate defensive location, can be tabled a bit as Dubon remains an advanced depth MLB roster consideration. The long view might stick Dubon as a second baseman, or perhaps as a high-end utility option; now we know that role is close to materializing.

YEAR	TEAM	LVL	AGE	PA	DRC+	VORP	BABIP	BRR	FRAA	WARP
2016	SLM	A+	21	279	138	25.6	.338	5.5	SS(61): -11.6	0.8
2016	PME	AA	21	270	143	25.7	.374	4.1	SS(62): -5.7	1.7
2017	BLX	AA	22	304	101	6.7	.319	0.3	SS(53): 5.4, 2B(20): 3.0	1.6
2017	CSP	AAA	22	244	74	0.3	.297	-0.4	SS(30): -1.0, 2B(27): 3.5	0.2
2018	CSP	AAA	23	114	107	10.6	.379	1.5	SS(23): 0.3, 2B(4): 0.6	0.7
2019	MIL	MLB	24	64	64	-0.1	.280	0.2	SS 0, 2B 1	0.0

Jake Gatewood INF

Born: 09/25/95 Age: 23 Bats: R Throws: R
Height: 6'5" Weight: 190 Origin: Round 1, 2014 Draft (#41 overall)

YEAR	TEAM	LVL	AGE	PA	R	2B	3B	HR	RBI	BB	K	SB	CS	AVG/OBP/SLG
2016	WIS	A	20	524	70	33	0	14	64	18	141	3	2	.240/.268/.391
2017	CAR	A+	21	470	66	36	1	11	53	43	132	7	5	.269/.340/.438
2017	BLX	AA	21	100	9	4	2	4	9	8	29	3	0	.239/.300/.457
2018	BLX	AA	22	388	45	19	1	19	59	28	114	2	0	.244/.302/.466
2019	MIL	MLB	23	251	23	11	0	9	30	10	84	1	0	.194/.225/.362

Breakout: 2% Improve: 7% Collapse: 0% Attrition: 5% MLB: 7%
Comparables: Brandon Allen, Donald Lutz, Joey Terdoslavich

Certainty is the last ingredient any prospect profile could possibly have, but it's the easiest ingredient to envision on the shelf. Gatewood gives this tempting promise, after the right-handed power bat acquitted himself well in his first full season attempt at the Southern League. Previously famous for retooling his swing and adding contact lenses to his repertoire, Gatewood went all-in with the game power, hitting for extra bases in more than 10 percent of his plate appearances. Only three other regular Southern League batters (300+ PA) accomplished that feat. The power will be crucial for Gatewood, as he played almost exclusively first base throughout 2018. Without a utility role, Gatewood must regularly tap into that power at the plate.

YEAR	TEAM	LVL	AGE	PA	DRC+	VORP	BABIP	BRR	FRAA	WARP
2016	WIS	A	20	524	89	3.9	.303	0.6	3B(93): -1.2, 1B(26): 0.5	-0.1
2017	CAR	A+	21	470	115	15.8	.364	-0.7	1B(80): 0.4, 3B(14): -0.1	0.4
2017	BLX	AA	21	100	89	2.7	.305	-0.1	3B(21): -0.4	-0.1
2018	BLX	AA	22	388	108	5.5	.299	-4.6	1B(87): 0.6, RF(2): -0.4	-0.4
2019	MIL	MLB	23	251	49	-11.2	.251	-0.4	1B 0, RF 0	-1.2

Keston Hiura 2B

Born: 08/02/96   Age: 22   Bats: R   Throws: R
Height: 5'11"   Weight: 190   Origin: Round 1, 2017 Draft (#9 overall)

YEAR	TEAM	LVL	AGE	PA	R	2B	3B	HR	RBI	BB	K	SB	CS	AVG/OBP/SLG
2017	BRR	RK	20	72	18	3	5	4	18	6	13	0	2	.435/.500/.839
2017	WIS	A	20	115	14	11	2	0	15	7	24	2	0	.333/.374/.476
2018	CAR	A+	21	228	38	16	3	7	23	14	47	4	6	.320/.382/.529
2018	BLX	AA	21	307	36	18	2	6	20	22	56	11	5	.272/.339/.416
2019	MIL	MLB	22	63	7	3	0	2	7	3	16	1	1	.237/.286/.390

Breakout: 17%   Improve: 41%   Collapse: 1%   Attrition: 21%   MLB: 45%
Comparables: Jonathan Schoop, Arismendy Alcantara, Ryan Brett

Against the old adage "greed is good," risk is better. It's the assessment of risk that often leads to pricing discrepancies, such as Hiura falling to the ninth spot of the 2017 draft. This was fantastic luck for the Brewers, who in failing to "tank" during their rebuild had to gamble just as much as anyone else in the 2017 draft. So Hiura fell, on (reasonable) health and positional concerns, but 2018 helped Hiura to demonstrate the "advanced" in that advanced college bat. Meanwhile, the positional concerns slowly wound down; Hiura played almost twice as many games at the keystone as he did at designated hitter. The 22-year-old even had a chance to assuage other adversities, as a thumb injury derailed much of the second half of his minor-league season. Fortunately, the Arizona Fall League exists for elite MLB-bound prospects like Hiura, and the bat came all the way back in that friendly hitting environment. Here risk is reward, with Hiura placing an exclamation point on his midseason status as one of the top prospects in the industry.

YEAR	TEAM	LVL	AGE	PA	DRC+	VORP	BABIP	BRR	FRAA	WARP
2017	BRR	RK	20	72	262	17.1	.500	0.5		0.7
2017	WIS	A	20	115	138	10.3	.422	1.1	2B(3): -0.4	0.5
2018	CAR	A+	21	228	159	20.8	.386	0.6	2B(15): 0.6	1.5
2018	BLX	AA	21	307	116	13.9	.323	0.6	2B(64): -3.5	0.5
2019	MIL	MLB	22	63	83	1.0	.291	0.0	2B -1	0.0

Tristen Lutz RF

Born: 08/22/98 Age: 20 Bats: R Throws: R
Height: 6'3" Weight: 210 Origin: Round 1, 2017 Draft (#34 overall)

YEAR	TEAM	LVL	AGE	PA	R	2B	3B	HR	RBI	BB	K	SB	CS	AVG/OBP/SLG
2017	HEL	RK	18	111	23	1	1	6	16	12	21	2	4	.333/.432/.559
2017	BRR	RK	18	76	12	4	3	3	11	4	21	1	0	.279/.347/.559
2018	WIS	A	19	503	63	33	3	13	63	46	139	9	3	.245/.321/.421
2019	MIL	MLB	20	251	22	8	1	8	23	7	91	0	0	.147/.171/.286

Breakout: 4% Improve: 4% Collapse: 0% Attrition: 2% MLB: 4%
Comparables: Chris Parmelee, Caleb Gindl, Nomar Mazara

The seasons of player development are plentiful. Clocks tick, leaves change and temperatures fluctuate as players wind toward their Overall Future Potential. Those seasons are often equally harsh judges: Lutz couldn't find the hit or power tools in the April cold of the Midwest League, and they vanished once more in the heat of August. Yet the hits sprung forward in May, and the mundane days of July were hardly monotonous for the big outfielder. These seasons change for an age-19 prospect playing their first full year, forging a path to a "true" right fielder. That path remains long, but thankfully the repetitions of player development can be as meaningful as seasonal returns; here, Lutz eagerly awaits April 2019.

YEAR	TEAM	LVL	AGE	PA	DRC+	VORP	BABIP	BRR	FRAA	WARP
2017	HEL	RK	18	111	141	11.5	.373	-1.1	CF(22): -1.7	0.3
2017	BRR	RK	18	76	119	3.9	.364	0.1	CF(11): 0.5, LF(4): -1.2	0.0
2018	WIS	A	19	503	115	13.1	.322	-0.9	RF(68): -11.4, LF(29): 1.9	-0.2
2019	MIL	MLB	20	251	16	-18.4	.190	-0.2	RF -3, LF -1	-2.4

Milwaukee Brewers 2019

Jacob Nottingham   C
Born: 04/03/95   Age: 24   Bats: R   Throws: R
Height: 6'2"   Weight: 230   Origin: Round 6, 2013 Draft (#167 overall)

YEAR	TEAM	LVL	AGE	PA	R	2B	3B	HR	RBI	BB	K	SB	CS	AVG/OBP/SLG
2016	BLX	AA	21	456	46	14	0	11	37	29	138	9	2	.234/.295/.347
2017	BLX	AA	22	385	37	21	2	9	48	37	87	7	3	.209/.326/.369
2018	MIL	MLB	23	24	2	1	0	0	0	4	8	0	0	.200/.333/.250
2018	CSP	AAA	23	196	33	10	2	10	36	14	59	2	1	.281/.347/.528
2019	MIL	MLB	24	32	3	1	0	1	3	2	10	0	0	.172/.250/.310

Breakout: 12%   Improve: 19%   Collapse: 0%   Attrition: 23%   MLB: 27%
Comparables: Andrew Knapp, Luke Montz, Michael McKenry

For all the effort a player makes to improve their shortcomings or solidify their strengths, then comes the certainty of the injury bug, trades or other role diversions. It was the injury bug that derailed Nottingham for much of 2018, especially disappointing given that the big catcher was on the verge of transferring his improved defensive profile to the MLB level. For years the scouting questions have narrowed in on Nottingham's ability to block pitches and perform behind the plate, and upon reaching the majors he looked the part. The power and plate discipline showed up at Triple-A in eye-popping form even suitable for the Pacific Coast League; Nottingham hardly had enough time in the big leagues to develop an approach, but he did walk twice and score a run in his April debut. This might be a first base profile when all is said and done, but entering his age-25 season Nottingham still has time to make some form of "catcher with pop" work.

YEAR	TEAM	P. COUNT	FRM RUNS	BLK RUNS	THRW RUNS	TOT RUNS
2017	BLX	11440	7.2	-1.7	0.0	5.8
2018	CSP	4056	1.5	-1.1	-0.2	0.0
2018	MIL	937	-0.7	0.2	0.0	-0.5
2019	MIL	1179	-0.2	-0.2	0.0	-0.5

YEAR	TEAM	LVL	AGE	PA	DRC+	VORP	BABIP	BRR	FRAA	WARP
2016	BLX	AA	21	456	77	12.2	.320	0.0	C(98): 4.2, 1B(3): 0.1	0.4
2017	BLX	AA	22	385	104	13.2	.255	-3.0	C(83): 4.7, 1B(13): -0.8	1.1
2018	MIL	MLB	23	24	71	0.7	.333	-0.1	C(8): -0.5	0.0
2018	CSP	AAA	23	196	96	10.7	.367	-0.6	C(32): -0.3, 1B(9): 0.0	0.3
2019	MIL	MLB	24	32	65	0.2	.270	0.0	C -1	-0.1

Corey Ray CF

Born: 09/22/94 Age: 24 Bats: L Throws: L
Height: 6'0" Weight: 195 Origin: Round 1, 2016 Draft (#5 overall)

YEAR	TEAM	LVL	AGE	PA	R	2B	3B	HR	RBI	BB	K	SB	CS	AVG/OBP/SLG
2016	BRV	A+	21	254	24	13	2	5	17	20	54	9	5	.247/.307/.385
2017	CAR	A+	22	503	56	29	4	7	48	48	156	24	10	.238/.311/.367
2018	BLX	AA	23	600	86	32	7	27	74	60	176	37	7	.239/.323/.477
2019	MIL	MLB	24	251	33	10	2	9	26	16	82	8	2	.193/.247/.371

Breakout: 13% Improve: 18% Collapse: 2% Attrition: 11% MLB: 24%
Comparables: Trayce Thompson, Melky Mesa, Matt Den Dekker

What's a fast-rising, no-questions-asked college bat anyway? Ray returned to the prospect scene in 2018 by producing a line that's impossible to ignore. Ray reportedly adjusted his swing and pitch recognition skills in order to unlock his big power, while also progressing in center field. It still looks like a risky profile in the advanced minors. Even with those developments, Ray is a big time swing-and-miss hitter, as that improved season at the plate found time for a strikeout rate near 30 percent. He's on track to debut at some point in 2019.

YEAR	TEAM	LVL	AGE	PA	DRC+	VORP	BABIP	BRR	FRAA	WARP
2016	BRV	A+	21	254	88	2.4	.299	-1.9	CF(40): -3.3	-0.7
2017	CAR	A+	22	503	97	8.0	.346	-2.5	CF(80): 5.5, RF(24): 0.9	0.6
2018	BLX	AA	23	600	118	35.8	.303	0.5	CF(126): 1.8, LF(6): 1.4	2.4
2019	MIL	MLB	24	251	64	-0.2	.249	1.2	CF 1, LF 0	0.1

Troy Stokes LF

Born: 02/02/96   Age: 23   Bats: R   Throws: R
Height: 5'8"   Weight: 182   Origin: Round 4, 2014 Draft (#116 overall)

YEAR	TEAM	LVL	AGE	PA	R	2B	3B	HR	RBI	BB	K	SB	CS	AVG/OBP/SLG
2016	WIS	A	20	366	50	20	4	4	29	36	62	20	4	.268/.358/.395
2017	CAR	A+	21	426	60	19	5	14	56	47	77	21	9	.250/.344/.445
2017	BLX	AA	21	153	19	9	0	6	18	16	34	9	3	.252/.333/.452
2018	BLX	AA	22	551	74	23	6	19	58	65	147	19	2	.233/.343/.430
2019	MIL	MLB	23	251	32	9	2	9	26	20	71	6	1	.194/.269/.361

Breakout: 10%   Improve: 23%   Collapse: 2%   Attrition: 13%   MLB: 27%
Comparables: Chad Huffman, Jordan Luplow, Thomas Neal

The main knock on Stokes has been easy enough to recite in a way that lulls the observer into forecasting a supposedly crystal clear role: his hit tool leaves questions about MLB upside. But the speedy outfielder just doesn't quit, and it's worth citing the scouting knocks that have fallen by the wayside: what seemed a certain 'tweener outfield role years ago now looks like an average arm and glove that could hold down each outfield position. The power was absent years ago, but Stokes has refined that line-drive swing into a lofty effort that delivers game power in the advanced minors. The 23-year-old continues to place exclamation points on his ability to develop at every point in his career, giving him a chance to emerge from the shadows of that bench role.

YEAR	TEAM	LVL	AGE	PA	DRC+	VORP	BABIP	BRR	FRAA	WARP
2016	WIS	A	20	366	126	11.3	.319	-1.2	LF(59): -2.3, CF(10): -0.3	1.1
2017	CAR	A+	21	426	118	21.5	.278	0.5	LF(84): 5.5	1.5
2017	BLX	AA	21	153	119	5.9	.292	-0.3	LF(34): 1.0, CF(1): 0.0	0.4
2018	BLX	AA	22	551	117	28.5	.295	-1.5	LF(114): 4.1, CF(9): -1.5	1.4
2019	MIL	MLB	23	251	73	0.2	.238	0.7	LF 3, CF 0	0.3

Brice Turang SS

Born: 11/21/99 Age: 19 Bats: L Throws: R
Height: 6'1" Weight: 165 Origin: Round 1, 2018 Draft (#21 overall)

YEAR	TEAM	LVL	AGE	PA	R	2B	3B	HR	RBI	BB	K	SB	CS	AVG/OBP/SLG
2018	BRR	RK	18	57	11	2	0	0	7	9	6	8	1	.319/.421/.362
2018	HEL	RK	18	135	26	4	1	1	11	22	28	6	1	.268/.385/.348
2019	MIL	MLB	19	251	22	4	0	4	16	14	68	3	1	.154/.199/.225

Breakout: 5% Improve: 7% Collapse: 0% Attrition: 4% MLB: 9%
Comparables: Gleyber Torres, Adalberto Mondesi, Elvis Andrus

There is nothing new under the sun. Ancient philosophers knew this even before divine figures walked the earth, so it stands to reason this lesson could be passed through generations to reach MLB scouts. Turang was a hype casualty in the 2018 draft, generator of much press about so-called "prospect fatigue," an indicator that the scouts took to the hills in search of the new and exciting, perhaps a new future to dream on, bigger tools or tools they had yet to see. But there is nothing new under the sun, as Turang demonstrated after falling to the 21st pick despite previously carrying a potential 1:1 pedigree as a prep standout. Turang might not necessarily have booming power or a flashy glove or phenomenal speed, but the polished prospect has enough of each to complement his hit tool and construct an overall middle infield future worth those big dreams.

YEAR	TEAM	LVL	AGE	PA	DRC+	VORP	BABIP	BRR	FRAA	WARP
2018	BRR	RK	18	57	157	4.5	.357	0.0	SS(12): 2.0	0.5
2018	HEL	RK	18	135	119	9.7	.345	1.7	SS(23): -0.1, 2B(5): -0.1	0.6
2019	MIL	MLB	19	251	11	-17.3	.192	0.0	SS 0, 2B 0	-1.9

Weston Wilson UT

Born: 09/11/94 Age: 24 Bats: R Throws: R
Height: 6'3" Weight: 195 Origin: Round 17, 2016 Draft (#501 overall)

YEAR	TEAM	LVL	AGE	PA	R	2B	3B	HR	RBI	BB	K	SB	CS	AVG/OBP/SLG
2016	HEL	RK	21	269	38	16	7	4	38	23	33	5	4	.318/.390/.498
2017	WIS	A	22	162	22	9	2	5	26	16	29	1	5	.277/.366/.475
2017	CAR	A+	22	288	26	11	1	3	27	16	80	3	0	.241/.298/.326
2018	CAR	A+	23	424	60	23	2	13	62	31	93	7	4	.274/.330/.446
2018	BLX	AA	23	49	5	1	0	1	3	3	7	1	1	.239/.286/.326
2019	MIL	MLB	24	251	21	8	0	7	26	9	69	1	1	.192/.226/.316

Breakout: 0% Improve: 1% Collapse: 0% Attrition: 1% MLB: 1%
Comparables: Russ Canzler, Joe Mahoney, Ben Paulsen

The Arizona Fall League is regarded as a showcase for top prospects, and in October 2018 the league featured a utility player by design. Defensive flexibility is no longer a buzzword, which catapults prospects like Wilson into difficult territory for role projection. Looking at Wilson's profile, a scout could focus on that little bit of pop and some discipline at the plate, but nothing is necessarily jumping out with the hit tool. If one views the AFL as a potential bridge to MLB, Wilson's defensive flexibility leaps out, as the run down the defensive spectrum began primarily with third base and second base in 2016, the infield corners in 2017, and 1B/LF/3B/2B in 2018. Working in an MLB environment where more roster spots may be designated for pitchers, it's not hard to squint at Wilson's proven utility role and notch that Overall Future Potential slightly higher.

YEAR	TEAM	LVL	AGE	PA	DRC+	VORP	BABIP	BRR	FRAA	WARP
2016	HEL	RK	21	269	148	26.4	.350	0.6	3B(41): -1.8, 2B(11): -1.5	1.0
2017	WIS	A	22	162	124	12.4	.318	-0.6	3B(26): 0.5, 1B(10): 1.4	0.7
2017	CAR	A+	22	288	73	-5.9	.333	-2.3	1B(42): -0.3, 3B(7): 0.5	-1.2
2018	CAR	A+	23	424	110	17.1	.325	3.1	1B(38): 0.9, LF(25): 4.7	1.5
2018	BLX	AA	23	49	85	0.6	.263	0.4	3B(8): 0.1, 1B(4): 0.2	0.0
2019	MIL	MLB	24	251	42	-11.8	.237	-0.4	1B 0, 3B 0	-1.2

Luke Barker RHP

Born: 03/11/92 Age: 27 Bats: R Throws: R
Height: 6'3" Weight: 230 Origin: Undrafted Free Agent, 2016

YEAR	TEAM	LVL	AGE	W	L	SV	G	GS	IP	H	HR	BB/9	K/9	K	GB%	BABIP
2017	WIS	A	25	1	4	5	22	0	31^2	30	2	2.3	9.7	34	47%	.329
2017	CAR	A+	25	1	1	1	12	0	22	24	2	2.5	5.7	14	35%	.306
2018	CAR	A+	26	6	4	20	46	0	61	47	3	2.4	9.3	63	44%	.275
2019	MIL	MLB	27	2	1	2	47	0	50	47	8	3.5	8.5	47	40%	.297

Breakout: 4% Improve: 5% Collapse: 3% Attrition: 5% MLB: 9%
Comparables: Rafael Martin, Guido Knudson, Brad Salmon

The first thing that jumps out is how much Barker looks like Jake Arrieta, which is important because there are not many righties with this particular stature in MLB. The beard is a nice touch, too. Milwaukee purchased Barker's rights from independent ball, and debuted the five-pitch righty in Single-A for the 2017 season. Almost everything has gone right for Barker in the low minors. It's hard to ignore his command of the strike zone, even if he's old for the competition, a relatively polished product with three years at Chico State preceding his independent league play. Barker struck out 26 percent of batters faced in 2018, and features a fly ball-oriented approach to be carefully watched. It's hard to get past the minor-league level, age and relief role, but Barker sure looks like an MLB pitcher.

YEAR	TEAM	LVL	AGE	WHIP	ERA	DRA	WARP	MPH	FB%	WHF	CSP
2017	WIS	A	25	1.20	2.84	3.50	0.5				
2017	CAR	A+	25	1.36	3.68	3.90	0.3				
2018	CAR	A+	26	1.03	2.21	3.27	1.2				
2019	MIL	MLB	27	1.32	4.52	5.20	-0.2				

Milwaukee Brewers 2019

Zack Brown   RHP
Born: 12/15/94   Age: 24   Bats: R   Throws: R
Height: 6'1"   Weight: 180   Origin: Round 5, 2016 Draft (#141 overall)

YEAR	TEAM	LVL	AGE	W	L	SV	G	GS	IP	H	HR	BB/9	K/9	K	GB%	BABIP
2016	WIS	A	21	1	2	1	9	4	33	29	3	1.4	7.9	29	45%	.257
2017	WIS	A	22	4	5	0	18	13	85	78	7	3.6	8.9	84	47%	.316
2017	CAR	A+	22	3	0	0	4	4	25	24	1	0.7	8.3	23	56%	.319
2018	BLX	AA	23	9	1	0	22	21	125^2	95	8	2.6	8.3	116	57%	.257
2019	MIL	MLB	24	6	6	1	32	17	102^2	91	13	3.2	8.2	94	46%	.289

Breakout: 16%   Improve: 23%   Collapse: 16%   Attrition: 35%   MLB: 48%
Comparables: Eric Jokisch, Steven Brault, Nick Kingham

One of the ongoing stories for the 2018 Brewers was their elite bullpen and a national perception that they needed rotation help. All of this overshadowed the club's systemic development of high-floor minor-league arms into functional units, getting pitchers to stick with what works despite potential scouting flaws that would limit promulgation of elite rotation role fantasies. Brown is but one example of the type of arm the Brewers developed in 2018, a college prospect pushed quickly beyond A-ball and challenged in the advanced minors, where that floor becomes apparent. One wouldn't expect Brown's blend of a solid low-90s fastball, breakers with changing shapes and a change of pace to blow away the scouting scene, and the delivery might obscure the appearances of a frame that can withstand a starter's workload. Still, Brown worked two consecutive seasons with more than 100 innings, producing a profile that deserves extended looks and questions about what a pitching role is, anyway.

YEAR	TEAM	LVL	AGE	WHIP	ERA	DRA	WARP	MPH	FB%	WHF	CSP
2016	WIS	A	21	1.03	3.00	5.40	-0.2				
2017	WIS	A	22	1.32	3.39	4.78	0.4				
2017	CAR	A+	22	1.04	2.16	3.35	0.6				
2018	BLX	AA	23	1.04	2.44	3.42	2.8				
2019	MIL	MLB	24	1.25	4.13	4.74	0.7				

Bubba Derby RHP

Born: 02/24/94 Age: 25 Bats: L Throws: R
Height: 5'11" Weight: 185 Origin: Round 6, 2015 Draft (#188 overall)

YEAR	TEAM	LVL	AGE	W	L	SV	G	GS	IP	H	HR	BB/9	K/9	K	GB%	BABIP
2016	BRV	A+	22	6	13	0	26	25	132	165	17	3.2	7.4	109	45%	.348
2017	BLX	AA	23	2	1	0	18	2	50	40	1	3.6	8.3	46	44%	.289
2017	CSP	AAA	23	5	0	0	12	12	63^1	59	7	2.4	7.0	49	50%	.286
2018	CSP	AAA	24	6	5	0	31	16	118^1	127	9	3.8	7.3	96	47%	.328
2019	MIL	MLB	25	6	6	1	38	17	100^1	93	14	3.7	8.4	93	44%	.298

Breakout: 8% Improve: 13% Collapse: 14% Attrition: 23% MLB: 31%
Comparables: Chad Bell, Stephen Fife, Hiram Burgos

One of the interesting aspects of watching The Age of Velocity in baseball is seeing which *impossible* slow throwers reach the majors and establish serviceable roles. Derby is one candidate for this type of hobby, as the righty hardly tops out near the league-median fastball. When the Athletics traded him to the Brewers he might have been organizational depth, and then he might have been a reliever when he moved to Double-A. Since these developments, Derby has used a modest, command-oriented approach while the Brewers provided a solid slate of starts at Triple-A, reorienting the righty's org depth prospects. Milwaukee rewarded Derby with an Arizona Fall League appearance, following a recent set of moves in which depth-based arms are sent to the premier prospect showcase, which solidifies his prospect status even if the exact role is difficult to pinpoint.

YEAR	TEAM	LVL	AGE	WHIP	ERA	DRA	WARP	MPH	FB%	WHF	CSP
2016	BRV	A+	22	1.61	5.59	5.60	-0.2				
2017	BLX	AA	23	1.20	2.88	3.36	0.9				
2017	CSP	AAA	23	1.20	3.55	4.36	0.9				
2018	CSP	AAA	24	1.50	4.49	5.22	0.3				
2019	MIL	MLB	25	1.34	4.46	5.12	0.0				

Milwaukee Brewers 2019

Marcos Diplan   RHP

Born: 09/18/96   Age: 22   Bats: R   Throws: R
Height: 6'0"   Weight: 170   Origin: International Free Agent, 2013

YEAR	TEAM	LVL	AGE	W	L	SV	G	GS	IP	H	HR	BB/9	K/9	K	GB%	BABIP
2016	WIS	A	19	6	2	1	17	11	70	49	3	4.1	11.4	89	51%	.274
2016	BRV	A+	19	1	2	0	10	6	43¹	47	4	3.7	8.3	40	39%	.333
2017	CAR	A+	20	7	8	0	26	22	125²	126	11	5.1	8.5	119	48%	.327
2018	CAR	A+	21	3	2	0	13	13	61¹	58	3	5.6	8.8	60	48%	.344
2018	BLX	AA	21	2	6	0	12	11	57	58	6	5.7	9.0	57	41%	.325
2019	MIL	MLB	22	1	1	0	21	0	22	20	3	5.9	9.8	25	42%	.296

Breakout: 8%   Improve: 11%   Collapse: 3%   Attrition: 12%   MLB: 14%
Comparables: Dallas Braden, Dellin Betances, John Gant

Milwaukee placed Diplan on the 40-man roster prior to the 2018 season, but the righty remained on a relatively slow path to the majors. We've been writing about him for years, so it's easy to forget that Diplan will work during his age-22 season in 2019, but the profile still seems stalled. He just completed three consecutive years with time in High-A, producing a total of 230 innings at that level. Once Diplan was promoted to Double-A, his ground-ball rate backed up while the whiffs and walks didn't budge much. The same caveats hold: command is the major concern with Diplan, even if the fastball is now more clearly grouped with a change and breaker.

YEAR	TEAM	LVL	AGE	WHIP	ERA	DRA	WARP	MPH	FB%	WHF	CSP
2016	WIS	A	19	1.16	1.80	2.91	1.7				
2016	BRV	A+	19	1.50	4.98	3.22	1.1				
2017	CAR	A+	20	1.57	5.23	5.30	-0.1				
2018	CAR	A+	21	1.57	3.52	3.79	1.1				
2018	BLX	AA	21	1.65	4.58	4.91	0.3				
2019	MIL	MLB	22	1.54	4.79	5.04	-0.1				

Thomas Jankins   RHP

Born: 07/02/95   Age: 23   Bats: R   Throws: R
Height: 6'3"   Weight: 200   Origin: Round 13, 2016 Draft (#381 overall)

YEAR	TEAM	LVL	AGE	W	L	SV	G	GS	IP	H	HR	BB/9	K/9	K	GB%	BABIP
2016	HEL	RK	20	0	0	0	4	2	11^2	12	2	1.5	10.8	14	52%	.323
2016	WIS	A	20	0	2	0	8	7	25^1	33	0	2.1	7.5	21	62%	.402
2017	WIS	A	21	9	8	0	27	24	141^2	141	14	2.0	7.7	121	55%	.305
2018	BLX	AA	22	10	9	0	23	21	130^1	130	13	2.5	6.6	95	50%	.302
2019	MIL	MLB	23	6	7	0	32	19	112^2	111	18	3.1	7.6	95	47%	.301

Breakout: 6%   Improve: 10%   Collapse: 11%   Attrition: 19%   MLB: 23%
Comparables: Felix Jorge, Zach Lee, Anthony Bass

What is a sleeper? So many minor leaguers will fade off before they reach the majors, hitting a role ceiling, experiencing an injury or simply dropping off at the wrong time in their development cycle. It's easy to find sleepers, then: there are so many players who could succeed *if only this or that goes right*. Jankins, on the other hand, is a sleeper by leaping over High-A and posting a better-than-average DRA for Double-A Biloxi. The righty did all this with an unassuming sinker and slider combo, focusing on movement and command to succeed without velocity. This makes Jankins an intriguing high-floor depth arm, and when the attrition of 162 games wears down other louder arms that dot prospect lists, "unassuming" can morph into "valuable."

YEAR	TEAM	LVL	AGE	WHIP	ERA	DRA	WARP	MPH	FB%	WHF	CSP
2016	HEL	RK	20	1.20	3.09	2.82	0.4				
2016	WIS	A	20	1.54	3.20	3.72	0.4				
2017	WIS	A	21	1.22	3.62	3.97	2.1				
2018	BLX	AA	22	1.27	4.42	4.01	2.0				
2019	MIL	MLB	23	1.34	4.70	5.41	-0.3				

Jimmy Nelson RHP

Born: 06/05/89 Age: 30 Bats: R Throws: R
Height: 6'6" Weight: 250 Origin: Round 2, 2010 Draft (#64 overall)

YEAR	TEAM	LVL	AGE	W	L	SV	G	GS	IP	H	HR	BB/9	K/9	K	GB%	BABIP
2016	MIL	MLB	27	8	16	0	32	32	179[1]	186	25	4.3	7.0	140	51%	.299
2017	MIL	MLB	28	12	6	0	29	29	175[1]	171	16	2.5	10.2	199	51%	.340
2019	MIL	MLB	30	6	5	0	16	16	84	75	9	3.2	9.4	88	49%	.293

Breakout: 16% Improve: 51% Collapse: 20% Attrition: 9% MLB: 93%
Comparables: Tyson Ross, Jeff Locke, Hyun-jin Ryu

Nelson had hoped to return in the second half, which would have made the already fun Brewers an even better story, but instead he ended up missing the entire 2018 season recovering from a September 2017 shoulder injury suffered while running the bases. Prior to his career being derailed, Nelson had taken major strides to become a potential front-line starter, thriving in 2017 even while the BABIP gods did him dirty. However, it's hard to predict how he'll fare after what will be nearly 18 months off by the time spring training rolls around.

YEAR	TEAM	LVL	AGE	WHIP	ERA	DRA	WARP	MPH	FB%	WHF	CSP
2016	MIL	MLB	27	1.52	4.62	6.23	-1.8	95.5	70.8	8.4	50.7
2017	MIL	MLB	28	1.25	3.49	3.32	4.4	95.5	61.2	12.3	50.7
2019	MIL	MLB	30	1.24	3.54	3.98	1.1	94.7	65.3	10.5	50.6

Cody Ponce RHP

Born: 04/25/94 Age: 25 Bats: R Throws: R
Height: 6'6" Weight: 240 Origin: Round 2, 2015 Draft (#55 overall)

YEAR	TEAM	LVL	AGE	W	L	SV	G	GS	IP	H	HR	BB/9	K/9	K	GB%	BABIP
2016	BRV	A+	22	2	8	0	17	17	72	84	6	2.1	8.6	69	47%	.345
2017	CAR	A+	23	8	8	0	22	22	120	130	14	1.9	7.1	94	42%	.312
2017	BLX	AA	23	2	1	0	3	3	17^2	10	0	2.5	4.6	9	54%	.200
2018	BLX	AA	24	7	6	0	29	11	95	88	10	3.2	8.3	88	45%	.294
2019	MIL	MLB	25	5	5	1	28	15	88^2	84	13	3.0	8.1	80	42%	.298

Breakout: 4% Improve: 6% Collapse: 7% Attrition: 14% MLB: 17%
Comparables: Ryan Carpenter, Jason Wheeler, Mike Wright

Witness the tortoise and the hare: Entering 2016, right handers Cody Ponce and Freddy Peralta represented two of the most divergent profiles in baseball. Peralta, a diminutive 20-year-old out of the Dominican Republic, made his first entry into full-season ball; Ponce, the definition of a big, advanced college arm, began the season in High-A and seemed poised to be a fast riser at age 22. The fast riser appeal seemed especially probable if one stuck with Ponce as a reliever or back-end starter. Ponce stalled. In 2017, the Brewers moved their High-A affiliate to Carolina, and so too moved Ponce, who finally earned a call to Double-A in late August of that year, catching up with the fast-rising Peralta. The slow-cooker continued with Ponce in 2018, when the underlying stats look solid, placing an exclamation point on the end of those fast-riser dreams. Now that back-end rotation role is a dream, but it feels entirely too soon to say that Ponce is close.

YEAR	TEAM	LVL	AGE	WHIP	ERA	DRA	WARP	MPH	FB%	WHF	CSP
2016	BRV	A+	22	1.40	5.25	3.57	1.6				
2017	CAR	A+	23	1.29	3.38	4.08	1.7				
2017	BLX	AA	23	0.85	1.53	5.39	0.0				
2018	BLX	AA	24	1.28	4.36	4.01	1.3				
2019	MIL	MLB	25	1.29	4.41	5.08	0.1				

Milwaukee Brewers 2019

Trey Supak RHP
Born: 05/31/96   Age: 23   Bats: R   Throws: R
Height: 6'5"   Weight: 235   Origin: Round 2, 2014 Draft (#73 overall)

YEAR	TEAM	LVL	AGE	W	L	SV	G	GS	IP	H	HR	BB/9	K/9	K	GB%	BABIP
2016	HEL	RK	20	1	1	0	4	2	14	10	0	0.6	7.1	11	54%	.256
2016	WIS	A	20	2	3	1	11	6	44^1	48	3	3.5	8.1	40	41%	.338
2017	WIS	A	21	2	2	0	8	7	41	21	1	2.2	11.6	53	36%	.235
2017	CAR	A+	21	3	4	1	15	11	72^1	65	12	3.5	7.1	57	34%	.261
2018	CAR	A+	22	2	1	0	9	9	51	37	2	2.8	8.5	48	38%	.269
2018	BLX	AA	22	6	6	0	16	16	86^2	74	4	2.9	7.8	75	45%	.286
2019	MIL	MLB	23	2	2	0	6	6	31	31	5	3.6	8.5	30	38%	.292

Breakout: 2%   Improve: 3%   Collapse: 14%   Attrition: 15%   MLB: 19%
Comparables: Adalberto Mejia, Steven Brault, Aaron Blair

Let's have some fun with the mid-rotation starter! In 2018, 299 pitchers made at least two starts in the majors. The 70th percentile cutoff was 132 2/3 innings, 24 starts, a 3.99 DRA and a 3.68 ERA. Below that threshold, how many pitchers truly need more than two workable pitches? What type of command or mechanical shortcomings are exhibited below this threshold? We ask on behalf of Supak, who many view as a relief prospect given the unsightly walk totals, plus a profile that mostly hinges on two pitches. Yet this is not to oversell the questions on Supak, as the big righty also yielded more ground balls after making the leap to Double-A. With a strong fastball-curve profile and two consecutive seasons with more than 100 innings, Supak looks like a mid-rotation arm in a league starved for innings and settling on lower workloads to fill out their starts.

YEAR	TEAM	LVL	AGE	WHIP	ERA	DRA	WARP	MPH	FB%	WHF	CSP
2016	HEL	RK	20	0.79	1.29	2.75	0.4				
2016	WIS	A	20	1.47	3.86	3.75	0.6				
2017	WIS	A	21	0.76	1.76	2.74	1.2				
2017	CAR	A+	21	1.29	4.60	4.41	0.7				
2018	CAR	A+	22	1.04	1.76	4.69	0.4				
2018	BLX	AA	22	1.18	2.91	3.73	1.6				
2019	MIL	MLB	23	1.34	4.60	5.12	0.0				

LINEOUTS

Hitters

HITTER	POS	TEAM	LVL	AGE	PA	R	2B	3B	HR	RBI	BB	K	SB	CS	AVG/OBP/SLG	DRC+	WARP
Larry Ernesto	RF	DBW	Rk	17	221	38	13	2	5	20	14	68	9	4	.236/.294/.394	72	0.8
Trent Grisham	OF	BLX	AA	21	405	45	10	2	7	31	63	87	11	3	.233/.356/.337	109	1.0
Erik Kratz	C	SWB	AAA	38	61	10	2	0	4	6	7	10	0	0	.269/.356/.538	128	0.6
	C	MIL	MLB	38	219	18	6	0	6	23	6	40	1	0	.236/.280/.355	91	2.0
Robie Rojas	C	CAR	A+	23	44	7	2	0	0	5	6	15	0	0	.351/.455/.405	128	0.2
Tyler Saladino	SS	CHA	MLB	28	9	2	1	0	0	0	0	3	0	0	.250/.250/.375	80	0.0
	SS	CSP	AAA	28	154	23	4	3	3	19	21	28	10	0	.262/.370/.408	102	0.3
	SS	MIL	MLB	28	130	11	3	0	5	16	9	38	2	2	.246/.302/.398	88	0.5
Tyrone Taylor	OF	CSP	AAA	24	481	73	23	9	20	80	27	74	13	4	.278/.321/.504	99	1.8

After signing a big bonus during the summer of 2017, international prospect **Larry Ernesto** has already reached the continent and flashed that bat during a short stint in Arizona. ⓥ Milwaukee signed a couple of international prospects to identical deals in 2018, but **Eduarqui Fernandez** should not be confused for a bat-first play. This outfielder could build a name on defense up the middle, depending on how his 6-foot-2 frame ages and fills out. ⓥ It was difficult not to lean on the name change for **Trent Grisham**, potentially a heartwarming narrative coupled with rejuvenation on the field. While climbing the ladder ever closer to MLB, the scouting knocks on the bat and power came along with Grisham. ⓥ Pour one out for the organizational catcher. **Dustin Houle** took five years to reach Double-A, bested that level, and absolutely shredded the Pacific Coast League for 13 plate appearances in 2018. How hard can you dream on a 50 arm? ⓥ Milwaukee is slowly increasing its presence around international baseball, with shortstop as their current success story. The club looks to **Branlyn Jaraba** as their next big-deal infielder, although this one probably moves down the defensive spectrum. ⓥ During the thrilling 2018 NLCS, a brief moment of organizational depth as performance art occurred when **Erik Kratz**'s college friends and teammates wore each of his previous MLB jerseys to Game 6. Kratz is truly blessed to have so many friends. ⓥ **Robie Rojas** dashed from the 38th round of the 2017 draft to Triple-A in 2018, which is about as thrilling as organizational depth gets. ⓥ The Brewers reacquainted **Tyler Saladino** with his leg kick in order to reclaim some of his previous power. While the homers resurfaced, Saladino's plate discipline leaves a new riddle for his next hitting coach. ⓥ From athletic top prospect to forgotten minor leaguer and back, **Tyrone Taylor** is evidence of the length of player development cycles. Now, the age-25 outfielder is young for Triple-A and has a chance to answer org depth questions.

Milwaukee Brewers 2019

Pitchers

PITCHER	TEAM	LVL	AGE	W	L	SV	G	GS	IP	H	HR	BB/9	K/9	K	GB%	WHIP	ERA	DRA	WARP
Matt Albers	MIL	MLB	35	3	3	1	34	0	34^1	45	10	3.1	8.4	32	47%	1.66	7.34	6.09	-0.5
Aaron Ashby	HEL	Rk	20	1	2	1	6	3	20^1	18	3	3.5	8.4	19	52%	1.28	6.20	4.37	0.3
	WIS	A	20	1	1	0	7	7	37^1	40	1	2.2	11.3	47	52%	1.31	2.17	2.86	1.0
Jacob Barnes	CSP	AAA	28	1	0	2	11	0	11^2	5	0	6.2	7.7	10	64%	1.11	1.54	4.11	0.1
	MIL	MLB	28	0	1	2	49	0	48^2	51	4	4.3	8.7	47	51%	1.52	3.33	3.54	0.8
Luis Gonzalez	BRR	Rk	19	1	2	0	7	2	11^1	15	2	10.3	4.8	6	43%	2.47	6.35	5.82	0.0
Jon Olczak	BLX	AA	24	10	3	4	42	0	56^1	36	1	2.9	9.6	60	41%	0.96	1.44	3.48	1.0
Miguel Sanchez	CAR	A+	24	1	0	1	10	0	21^1	14	4	2.5	12.7	30	53%	0.94	2.53	2.12	0.7
	BLX	AA	24	1	1	1	23	0	41	32	3	3.1	13.6	62	45%	1.12	2.63	1.95	1.4
Quintin Torres-Costa	BLX	AA	23	1	2	2	21	0	31	17	0	3.8	12.8	44	48%	0.97	1.16	2.90	0.7
	CSP	AAA	23	2	0	2	22	0	24	10	0	4.5	7.9	21	52%	0.92	1.50	4.16	0.3
Bobby Wahl	NAS	AAA	26	3	2	11	34	1	39^2	17	2	3.9	14.7	65	42%	0.86	2.27	1.43	1.7
	NYN	MLB	26	0	1	0	7	0	5^1	9	2	6.8	11.8	7	17%	2.44	10.12	4.11	0.0
Aaron Wilkerson	MIL	MLB	29	0	1	0	3	1	9	12	4	3.0	10.0	10	31%	1.67	10.00	6.02	-0.1
	CSP	AAA	29	4	5	0	15	12	72^1	64	3	3.1	7.6	61	42%	1.23	2.49	5.47	0.0
Taylor Williams	MIL	MLB	26	1	3	0	56	0	53	53	6	4.2	9.7	57	39%	1.47	4.25	4.34	0.4

Matt Albers had one of the most uneven run prevention seasons of 2018, shifting from elite early months to terrible performances after a run-in with the injury bug. ⚾ Emerging from Crowder College in Missouri, lefty **Aaron Ashby** had the Brewers' scouting department clicking their heels across the Midwest in an effort to repeat their Corbin Burnes magic. This wizard offers three high-floor pitches, making him a junior college sleeper. ⚾ Once compared to Chuck Crim for a bread-and-butter fastball-slider profile, righty **Jacob Barnes** seemingly disappeared in 2018. Things mostly clicked in September even if the command didn't, raising questions about repeating those high-leverage scenarios of years past. ⚾ Everything seemed on the up-and-up for **Oliver Drake** and the Brewers, until the Reds battered him for six runs on six hits, all on pitches outside the strike zone. It quickly became apparent that this might not have been his year. ⚾ A projection righty from Puerto Rico, **Luis Gonzalez** escaped the pre-draft hype machine but was promising enough to be drafted in the eighth round. Gonzalez was one of three players drafted out of PJ Education School in 2018. ⚾ Organizational righty **Jon Olczak** made the leap to the advanced minors in 2018, earning a spot in the Arizona Fall League to boot. DRA likes Olczak, and he was also a run-prevention sensation in a dozen AFL innings. ⚾ Rehabbing college right-hander **Drew Rasmussen** fell from the 31st pick in 2017 to a sixth-round gamble in 2018, providing the Brewers with one of the high-risk fliers to potentially define the high end of their class. ⚾ Don't scout the stat line unless an organizational depth reliever like **Miguel Sanchez** increases his strikeouts by 44 percent while moving from Single-A to Triple-A in one season. Then send that player to the Arizona Fall League, and join the nameless, faceless reliever revolution. ⚾ Isn't it ironic, don't you think? It's like **Quintin Torres-Costa** being scouted as a LOOGY from the get go, and then getting injured upon completing Triple-A. ⚾ The "prize" of the lopsided Jeurys Familia trade, **Bobby Wahl** has an injury history that would make Mets' trainers squeal, which puts a bit of a damper on his huge minor-league strikeout rates and triple-digit heat. ⚾ When Michael Lewis writes a countercultural pitching tome *Brewers Guys*, **Aaron Wilkerson** will feature prominently. Perhaps a poor man's Mike Fiers, Wilkerson checks all the boxes: old prospect, taller than six feet, can't crack 90. ⚾ Once one of the most electric arms in the Brewers system, **Taylor Williams** has returned from an extended Tommy John episode to hold down the middle innings, from setup man to garbage time. When pitchers are throwing 120 mph in another decade or so, someone will fondly look back and ask, "Where have all the Taylor Williamses gone?"

Brewers Prospects

The State of the System:
While the Brew Crew did edge out the Cubs in the NL Central last year, they are going to fall just short of them in our org rankings. We don't think they'll mind.

The Top Ten:

1

Keston Hiura 2B   OFP: 70   Likely: 60   ETA: Late 2019
Born: 08/02/96   Age: 22   Bats: R   Throws: R   Height: 5'11"   Weight: 190
Origin: Round 1, 2017 Draft (#9 overall)

The Report: Hiura started his season 1-16 with five strikeouts and by my second chat of the year, people were clearly concerned. There's a song for that. Over the rest of the season, Hiura mashed. He then mashed in Fall Ball. And he's going to continue to mash. Although it doesn't usually draw superlatives for its aesthetic qualities, Hiura has a nearly perfect swing. Yes, there is a fairly significant leg kick for timing purposes, but the swing has Swiss-pocket-watch precision once he starts. Oh, and there's the matter of the plus bat speed married to a remarkably advanced approach. There's more raw power here than you might expect too. It's average, maybe even a smidge above, and you'd expect Hiura to get to almost all of it.

The bat will carry the profile here, but we have heard far fewer concerns about Hiura staying at the keystone lately. He's unlikely to be much more than average there, but he should be average there. The real show here is in the batter's box anyway, where he could be a perennial .300 hitter with a few 20-home-run seasons mixed in to boot.

  The Risks: Medium. There's little to quibble with here, but you'd like to see Hiura more thoroughly mash upper minors pitching at the outset of the 2019 season, and the defensive side of his game—while we are far more confident he's a long term second baseman than this time last year—still bears watching.

Bret Sayre's Fantasy Take:
  reads comments above
  takes deep exhale Yeeaaaaaaah that's the stuff.
  Hiura is just a hitter through and through. If all goes according to plan, he should be able to approximate the fantasy stats of Anthony Rendon—and do it from a middle infield spot.

Milwaukee Brewers 2019

2 **Tristen Lutz OF**   OFP: 60   Likely: 50   ETA: 2021
Born: 08/22/98   Age: 20   Bats: R   Throws: R   Height: 6'3"   Weight: 210
Origin: Round 1, 2017 Draft (#34 overall)

The Report: Athletic and strong, Lutz has the loudest tools of anyone on this list. Plus raw power and a strong throwing arm give him the profile of a future right fielder. At the plate he's got a quick, violent swing that has a swing path ideal for getting the ball in the air. He had trouble recognizing and adjusting to secondary pitches early on last year, but looked more comfortable as the season wore on.

Lutz is an exceptional athlete who can handle centerfield, but his future lies in right. He moves well for a big man, showing good instincts and range. The arm is strong and accurate and will be more than enough for any outfield spot. He's an above-average runner now but will probably slip to fringe-average as he matures physically. On the bases, he's not a burner but is aggressive enough to put pressure on defenders. The overall skill set is good with no tool projected to be below-average. It's the power potential that gives Lutz such a high ceiling, one that makes him stand out in a shallow Brewers' system.

The Risks: High. He's got a good base of skills but there are still some questions with bat and has yet to face advanced pitching.

Bret Sayre's Fantasy Take: If you're into a risk/reward profile, Lutz is for you. The thunder is real, but there are real questions as to how much of it he'll get to at peak, which would leave him more in the range of a .250 hitter with 30 homers. With a little speed to boot, Lutz is certainly a top-150 fantasy prospect right now and could easily make a notable jump in 2019 if he can make strides in his approach in High-A.

3 **Zack Brown RHP**   OFP: 55   Likely: 45   ETA: 2019
Born: 12/15/94   Age: 24   Bats: R   Throws: R   Height: 6'1"   Weight: 180
Origin: Round 5, 2016 Draft (#141 overall)

The Report: Brown had a breakout year in 2018, although granted, the organization did help clear a path for him. He's a shorter, slight right-hander with some effort in his arm action, but it does spit out low-90s heat with some sink and run that he effectively spots down more often than not. Brown will flash an above-average curveball and changeup as well. The curve can show with inconsistent shape or command, but at it's best it's a power 11-6 breaker. The change works well off the fastball with similar fade and depth and he sells the pitch well.

There's nothing overpowering here. Brown's command may never be much past average and his fastball is hittable up in the zone. Still, he's a polished three-pitch arm with some upper minors success under his belt. It'd be a breakout in better systems too.

The Risks: Medium. We're always gonna feel a little weird when projecting a short righty with some effort as a starter, but Brown has been relatively durable as a minor-league starter, and already has three advanced offerings. It's not huge upside, but he's a useful pitcher who should be ready this season. And he doesn't even have to pitch in Colorado Springs first.

Bret Sayre's Fantasy Take: Deeper leagues and certainly NL-only formats are places where Brown, and his ilk, can be most valuable. In mixed leagues, his brand of "SP5 in a poor ballpark" is one that can be replicated many times over for free during a given season. He's only worth worrying about at this point if your league rosters more than 200 prospects.

4. Corey Ray   OF
OFP: 55   Likely: 45   ETA: Late 2019/Early 2020
Born: 09/22/94   Age: 24   Bats: L   Throws: L   Height: 6'0"   Weight: 195
Origin: Round 1, 2016 Draft (#5 overall)

The Report: The series of unfortunate events that seemed to plague Ray since he was a top-five draft pick finally came to an end in 2018. Well, sort of. Ray played a full, healthy season and did more than just flash the power/speed combo that made him a top amateur prospect in the first place. He's added some loft to his swing and his well-documented raw power turned into significant game power. The speed is back from knee surgery and he has a shot to be an every day center fielder.

Ray always drew a wide range of projections, even dating back to his time in college. Last season was the first time he hit at all as a pro—as a 23-year-old in Double-A. That performance also came saddled with a ~30% K-rate and a swing long enough to preclude any significant future swing-and-miss improvement in its current form. His below-average hit tool may also limit how much of his plus raw power gets into games. Ultimately, Ray kept the flicker of an athletic 20/20 center fielder dream alive in 2018, but the three true outcome Double-A mashers aren't always great bets to maintain that performance in the majors.

The Risks: High. Ray has always been a risky one, and despite some performance gains in 2018, there's still significant hit tool/tweener risk.

Bret Sayre's Fantasy Take: I should really want to jump back in on Ray. We're talking about a former high-end draft pick who just hit nearly 30 homers and stole nearly 40 bases in Double-A two years after entering pro ball. We should all be excited, yet we're not. The hit tool is just too unlikely to allow the homers or the steals to matter. I'm not saying you should give up on him, but he's not a Top 101 fantasy prospect for me.

5. Brice Turang   SS
OFP: 55   Likely: 45   ETA: 2022
Born: 11/21/99   Age: 19   Bats: L   Throws: R   Height: 6'1"   Weight: 165
Origin: Round 1, 2018 Draft (#21 overall)

The Report: Turang slid down draft boards before the Brewers popped him with the 21st overall pick last June. A prep shortstop who is likely to stick at shortstop is never going to fall all that far, and Turang has the tools to be solid or better at the 6. Turang is an above-average runner who moves well in the field, and he shows good infield actions and enough arm for the left side of the dirt. He's not a surefire can't miss shortstop glove, but he's near the top of the "maybe" bucket.

The glove may have to be the carrying tool here, because it is tougher to see one at the plate. Turang steps in the bucket a bit, and his swing emphasizes contact with a slashy approach. None of this lends itself to consistently driving the ball. That—coupled with his smaller build—also limits any power projection, so he's going to have to find infield holes enough to hit .280 or so to be an above-average regular. Not impossible, but we are a long way off from that at present.

The Risks: High. Short-season resume with questions about how the bat will play at higher levels. Probably a shortstop isn't "a shortstop."

Bret Sayre's Fantasy Take: Sometimes when players fall in the draft, it's because of defensive questions. That's unfortunately not the case here. Turang may have somewhat limited upside from a fantasy standpoint, but he does have the contact ability to hit for a good average and steal 25-30 bases. There's also not zero power. It's basically a Jose Peraza profile with a little less speed. There's enough there to make him a solid third-round pick in dynasty drafts this year.

6   **Mauricio Dubon**   **IF**   OFP: 50   Likely: 45   ETA: 2019
Born: 07/19/94   Age: 24   Bats: R   Throws: R   Height: 6'0"   Weight: 160
Origin: Round 26, 2013 Draft (#773 overall)

The Report: Would a healthy Dubon have stopped the Brewers from needing to go out and trade for every infielder available at the 2018 deadline? Well, that's a bit hyperbolic, but he at least would have provided useful depth. Dubon has never quite recaptured the magic of that summer in Portland when he slugged .538, but he's stayed on pace to be a good fifth infielder/second-division starter type all along. A speedy middle infield type with experience at three infield spots—and even a brief center field run in the 2016 Arizona Fall League—Dubon is a nifty reserve in this era of small benches. He's never going to be much of a power hitter, and his bat control has covered for issues with spin at times, but assuming he returns more or less fit from his knee injury, Dubon should be a useful cog during Milwaukee's next playoff run.

The Risks: Low, but not actually low. Dubon was major-league-ready when he tore his ACL and he's a fairly low variance "good utility type," but that lack of risk was predicated on him being a speedy middle infielder type. Now he's one that just blew out his knee, so…

Bret Sayre's Fantasy Take: Mixed leaguers can pass here, as much as Matt Collins might object to me saying that. Dubon looks like a utility guy through and through, leaving him as a pretty valuable NL-only play, but a wanting one everywhere else.

7. Troy Stokes OF

OFP: 50   Likely: 40   ETA: Late 2019/Early 2020
Born: 02/02/96   Age: 23   Bats: R   Throws: R   Height: 5'8"   Weight: 182
Origin: Round 4, 2014 Draft (#116 overall)

The Report: In some ways the outfield version of Dubon—plus a couple grades of pop to be fair—Stokes is another in the long line of Brewers speed/power outfield prospects with hit tool questions. You could also call him stocky Corey Ray I suppose, although he lacks Ray's premium athleticism. Stokes does offer a broad base of defensive skills, enough to play all three outfield spots, along with some sneaky pull power. He can get into pull mode a bit too much, and the present issues with spin suggest a below-average hit tool long term, but he projects as a useful MLB bench piece.

The Risks: Medium. There's a chance the hit tool just doesn't get there and he's more of an up-and-down type.

Bret Sayre's Fantasy Take: This is just not a profile that ends well in dynasty leagues. Use the roster spot someone else. Anyone else will do.

8. Joe Gray OF

OFP: 50   Likely: 40   ETA: 2023
Born: 03/12/00   Age: 19   Bats: R   Throws: R   Height: 6'1"   Weight: 195
Origin: Round 2, 2018 Draft (#60 overall)

The Report: Gray is a projection pick with a right fielder's arm and raw power. The height and weight listed above are probably a fair bit light on both accounts already, and he's still got plenty of room to fill out and add strength. The overall profile at the plate is quite raw at present and the swing can get tentative and mechanical outside of batting practice. He's playing center for now, but he's probably a right fielder at the end of the day. Still, there are five potential tools here, and Gray provides a much needed shot of upside in a shallow system.

The Risks: High. Gray is a projection bet with only a complex-league resume and hit tool questions.

Bret Sayre's Fantasy Take: Gray barely registered on my top 50 signees from 2018, but the fact that he showed up at all means he's a worthy 4th or 5th round flier. It's far more tools than anything else, as you'd expect, but with the specter of above-average power and speed to at least match that, there are far worse profiles to gamble on.

9. Mario Feliciano C

OFP: 50   Likely: 40   ETA: 2021
Born: 11/20/98   Age: 20   Bats: R   Throws: R   Height: 6'1"   Weight: 195
Origin: Round 2, 2016 Draft (#75 overall)

The Report: Last year we ranked Feliciano in the next ten and wrote "Do expect him to occupy the space further up this list in the coming years." Well, we were right, but not for the right reasons. He missed most of 2018 with arm issues that eventually required offseason shoulder surgery. It was all but a lost season for the 19-year-old, who struggled even when on the field. The lost reps are concerning given the work Feliciano still needs to do on the defensive end, but he remains an athletic, potential bat-first backstop with time on his side… for now.

The Risks: High. Catchers are weird. Prep catchers are weirder. And this prep catcher might not hit.

Bret Sayre's Fantasy Take: Man, if you think I'm hard on catching prospects who have somewhat of a track record, just wait until you see how hard I am on ones who don't.

10 Lucas Erceg   3B   OFP: 50   Likely: 40   ETA: 2020
Born: 05/01/95   Age: 24   Bats: L   Throws: R   Height: 6'3"   Weight: 210
Origin: Round 2, 2016 Draft (#46 overall)

The Report: We liked Erceg a fair bit coming out of the draft, but his OFP has dropped precipitously as he's struggled to bring his plus raw power into games. Now he's a 23-year-old coming off a Double-A season where he posted an OPS under .700. Life comes at you fast and all that.

The culprit here isn't too tricky to identify. Erceg's swing is a bit long and a bit awkward coming from a closed off stance. He has enough control of the barrel to avoid big strikeout issues, but the quality of his contact has suffered, and he's always had an aggressive approach at the plate. He's a solid defensive third baseman with a big arm, but you have to hit at that corner infield spot too.

The Risks: High. Would you be surprised to learn this is another Brewers prospect with hit tool questions?

Bret Sayre's Fantasy Take: I'm completely out here. Erceg just doesn't have the offensive potential to be a top-250 prospect anymore. I'd rather gamble on about 50 complex league guys hoping to catch lightning in a bottle.

Other of note:

Drew Rasmussen, RHP, Did not pitch
Rasmussen was a first-round pick in 2017, but failed to come to an agreement with the Rays, and a fall Tommy John surgery—his second—has kept him on the shelf since. The Brewers took a flyer on him in the sixth round of this year's draft, and he showed a potential plus fastball along with two average secondaries at Oregon State when healthy. He hasn't been healthy in a very long while though, but in a system this shallow, he's a mere season away from a place on the Top 10's. That's a, uh, significant ask though, so check back this time next year.

Top Talents 25 and Under (born 4/1/93 or later):

1. Keston Hiura
2. Josh Hader
3. Corbin Burnes
4. Orlando Arcia
5. Brandon Woodruff
6. Tristen Lutz
7. Freddy Peralta
8. Zack Brown
9. Corey Ray
10. Brice Turang

Not 400 days ago, the Brewers looked like a team of the future. Now, they're living in the present, as recent success and this under-25 list will affirm. A club with less urgency wouldn't have dealt away high-variance, high-potential youngsters like Lewis Brinson, Monte Harrison and Isan Diaz. That club also wouldn't have nabbed blossoming NL MVP Christian Yelich, who just turned 27. So this thin list doesn't give a full picture of the organization's overall health, but does hint at where to watch for movement.

Hader and Burnes were pushed into relief roles to fill pressing holes on the big-league roster. Hader couldn't have been more suited for the role, while Burnes looked very "getting some reps and biding his time before trying the rotation." That's not a negative, either. Burnes' profile won't blow you away with upside, but could solid command and a more nuanced, versatile slider fuel him to No. 3 starter status? Sure!

Everyone just saw Hader's peak. If that wasn't the best he'll ever be, it was darn close—ideally he approximates that a few more times, and is a very good bullpen piece in seasons where his control falters. Both pitchers are important parts of the Brewers' core, but neither matches the potential impact of Hiura, who projects as a premier player at an up-the-middle position. No shame in that.

Orlando Arcia remains in a bit of a holding pattern. If he can summon even half of his postseason hitting ability, he's ranked too low here. That's not a statement made lightly—he's an impact shortstop defensively. The bat really needs to return to 2017 form, though, and it's anyone's guess on whether that'll be in the cards. If his feeble 2018 numbers prove to be the norm, he'll probably get lapped on this list by 2020.

Brandon Woodruff and Freddy Peralta live in a similar space. Of the two, Woodruff had loftier billing as a prospect, and he's proven he can miss bats and eat innings at the highest level. Peralta had some impressive moments of his own during his maiden big-league voyage, but he's almost entirely reliant on a magic fastball. It sits 90-92 and somehow still evades hitters in heavy, heavy doses. It would almost be more of a surprise if his schtick did hold up through multiple spins around the league. For now, proof of concept keeps him above Zack Brown's more diverse starter's repertoire.

Part 3: Featured Articles

The Hole in The Shift is Fixing Itself

Russell Carleton

I've been on a bit of a mission against The Shift of late. I'm not out to get The Shift for the usual reasons that people oppose it. The words "the right way to play the game" won't be found on my lips. If a team wants to pursue a strategy that is within the rules and it works, then by all means, they have my blessing (not that they need it). Instead, my concern with The Shift is a worry that it doesn't work, or at least that it has a flaw that needs fixing.

The data show that while The Shift does a decent job of preventing singles on balls in play (what it's supposed to do), it also increases the number of walks that happen in front of it, and the number of additional walks outweighs the number of singles saved. It's a problem because you can't throw a guy out if he gets to walk to first base.

But the "why" was important. It seemed that The Shift was changing the way in which pitchers pitched. We saw that there were fewer fastballs thrown in front of The Shift than we might otherwise expect, and that pitchers tended to stay out of the strike zone a little more. Not by a lot. In fact, it might not even be visible to the naked eye. The percentage of pitches that are out of the zone goes from 51.0 to 53.3 from a standard defense (two right/two left) to a full shift (three on one side). That difference stands up even after we control for the types of hitters that get shifted against. And it's enough to drive up the walk rate to where it cancels out the benefits that teams thought they were getting with The Shift… and then some.

But there was some hope. I found that when individual pitchers stayed closer to the in-zone/out-of-zone mix that they used without The Shift on, they could still get the benefits of The Shift without the walk problems. So, in theory, a team could simply figure out a way to convince its pitchers to not fall prey to the walk trap and The Shift would once again be their friend.

It's reasonable to think that some teams might be more hip to this idea than others. Maybe some figured it out a year before the others. Maybe they were better at getting the message across to their pitchers. Or, maybe no one has figured it out yet.

Warning! Gory Mathematical Details Ahead!

I used data from 2015-2017, made available through MLB's data portal, Baseball Savant. They are kind enough to note when teams are using an infield shift (three fielders on one side of second base), as opposed to a "strategic shift" (someone's playing a bit out of position, but it's not quite that drastic) or a "standard" alignment.

Since we're doing this by team, I can't just look at raw walk rates, because we know that some teams have good pitchers and others have not-so-good pitchers. Some have a mix of both. I used the log-odds ratio method to take into account a batter's general walking proclivities, and a pitcher's as well, and then shoving them into a binary logistic regression. Then, I asked the computer to generate a specific coefficient for each team's pitchers, for when they went into The Shift and how that affected their walk rate.

Using those coefficients, I was able to project what would happen if a league-average pitcher faced a league-average hitter (which we expect would product a league-average walk rate; from 2015-2017, 7.7 percent of plate appearances ended in a walk) and then just switched his hat. Here's the top five and the bottom five:

Top 5 Teams	Projected Shift Walk Rate	Bottom 5 Teams	Projected Shift Walk Rate
Rockies	6.2%	Rangers	11.2%
Pirates	6.7%	Mets	10.4%
Indians	7.2%	Dodgers	10.2%
Astros	7.3%	Cardinals	9.9%
Braves	7.7%	Tigers	9.7%

There are probably people out there right now trying to figure out what the common thread is among the top and bottom teams. I'm sure, because this is Baseball Prospectus, people are already trying to make the case that sabermetric "early adopters" have some sort of edge here. I think that the more interesting piece is that by the time you get to fifth place in The Shift, we're at league average.

As a sanity check, I examined the issue on a pitch-by-pitch level, looking at how often pitchers threw their pitches in the GameDay strike zone, and again using the same basic methodology and getting team-specific coefficients. The names on the list re-arranged themselves, but the idea was the same, and the two lists correlated with an R of .593.

There's a reason that I don't usually do this type of leaderboard post. I don't really know what the Rockies, Pirates, Indians, Astros, and Braves have in common, or what they have that the bottom five don't. I can put a shrug emoji here and say, "Well, it must be something!" but that seems like a cop-out. Instead, I'd like to present another table and suggest that the table above doesn't even really matter anymore.

Year	League Percent Outside K Zone (Full Shift)	League Percent in K Zone (No Shift)	Difference
2015	54.1%	51.1%	3.0%
2016	53.3%	50.9%	2.4%
2017	52.6%	50.9%	1.7%
2018	52.0%	50.7%	1.3%

The hole in The Shift is fixing itself, and it's coming down really fast league wide. In my earlier work on The Shift, I suggested that until teams stopped having such a huge difference between their out-of-zone rate with and without The Shift on, there would just be too many walks for The Shift to make sense. It seems that all 30 of them have been working toward just that. I once estimated that it takes about 10 years for an idea to filter its way through baseball. At this rate, it looks like teams are going to catch up a lot faster than that. And yeah, they're all saber-smart now.

It's likely that whatever magic it was that the Rockies and Pirates had has made its way to Texas and Queens. Or is at least on its way. And if teams are committing to fixing the walk problem, then it's likely that they will continue shifting and shifting a lot.

And eventually it's going to actually make sense for them to do it.

—*Russell Carleton is a former author of Baseball Prospectus and now an analyst for the New York Mets.*

The State of the Quality Start

Rob Mains

One of the seven things you (probably) didn't know about the 2018 season is that quality starts—defined as a start lasting six or more innings with three or fewer earned runs allowed—as a percentage of total starts cratered to an all-time low of 41 percent. I want to look a little more deeply into this, since it's been a while (May of 2016, to be exact) since I've examined quality starts.

The term *quality start* is credited to *Philadelphia Inquirer* sportswriter John Lowe. It's been derided ever since he coined it in December of 1985. Three runs in six innings? That's a 4.50 ERA! In what world is that a measure of quality?

Let's start with that criticism. It's true that 3 x 9 / 6 = 4.5. (You came here for this sort of high-level math, right?) But it's also true that type of start, meeting the bare minimum for earning a quality start, is unusual. Here's the proportion of quality starts in which the pitcher lasted exactly six innings and yielded exactly three earned runs. (I'm going to confine this analysis to the 30-team era, 1998-present. Almost all data retrieved in this article is via the Baseball-Reference Play Index.)

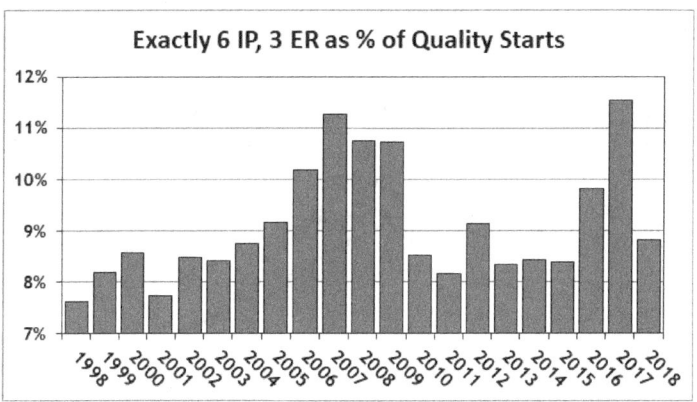

There were 1,997 quality starts in 2018. Only 176, or fewer than one in 11, featured a pitcher going six innings and allowing three earned runs. Put another way, the percentage of quality starts that resulted in a 4.50 ERA (8.8 percent) is less than half the percentage of games in which a batter hit two home runs and his team lost (22.5 percent; 237-69 won-lost). That doesn't impugn hitting two homers.

So if a 4.50 ERA isn't the norm, what is? How good are quality starts?

Pretty good, it turns out. First, on a team level:

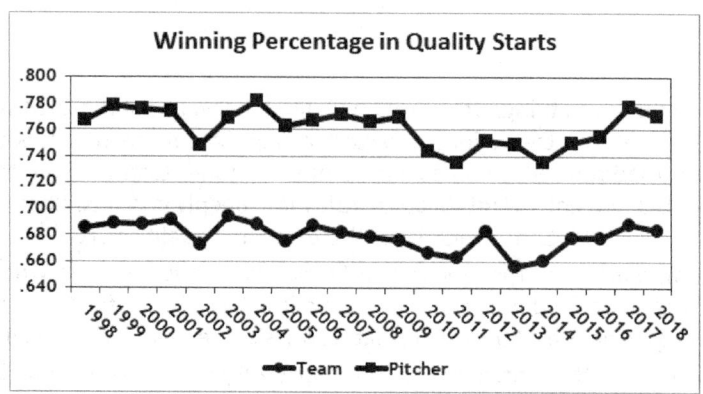

Teams receiving a quality start from their pitcher won 68.4 percent of their games in 2018, in line with the 30-team era average of 67.9 percent. A team with a .684 winning percentage wins 111 games. Getting a quality start is definitely a good thing. Individual pitchers throwing quality starts have a higher winning percentage because a big slice of team losses is assigned to a reliever.

If teams do well in quality starts, how well do the starting pitchers do? Again, very well.

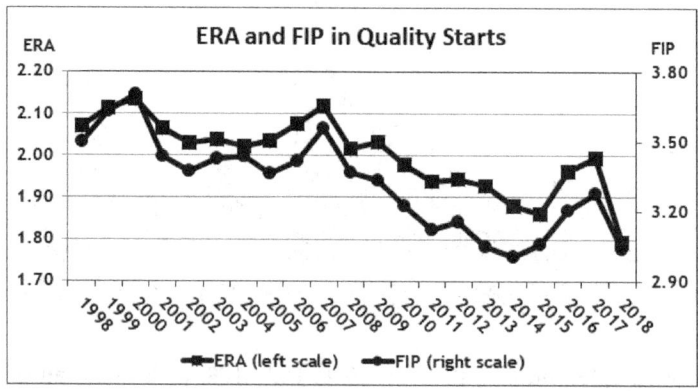

Pitchers in quality starts had a 1.79 ERA (blue line) in 2018, *the lowest in the 30-team era*. Their FIP was higher, 3.04, but still excellent. In the 30-team era, only 2014 had a lower FIP for quality starts, 3.01.

But, of course, the run environment in 2014 was different. Teams in 2014 scored 4.07 runs per game, the fewest in a non-strike year since 1976. They scored 4.45 runs per game in 2018. So surrendering a 3.04 FIP in 2018 is more impressive than 3.01 in 2014. Accordingly, let's look at ERA and FIP in quality starts relative to league averages.

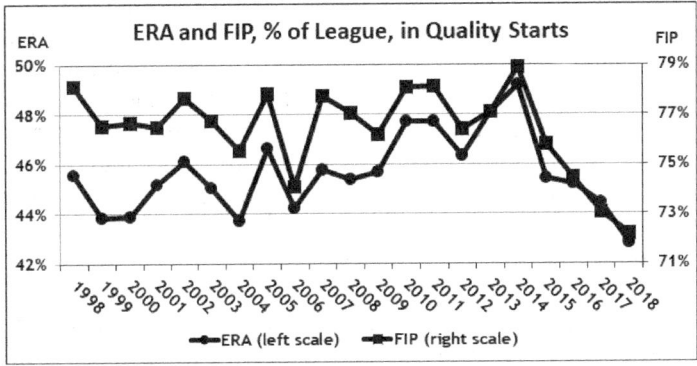

This tells a more dramatic story. Starting pitchers in 2018 gave up a 4.19 ERA and a 4.21 FIP. Starters in quality starts gave up a 1.79 ERA, 43 percent of the league average. Starters in quality starts gave up a 3.04 FIP, 72 percent of the league average. Both of these marks represent lows in the 30-team era.

The takeaway here is this: *Quality starts are better, relative to other starts, than they've ever been over the past 21 years.*

Maybe during the winter I'll look at this over a longer arc of time. For now, though, we can definitively say quality starts are the best they've ever been since the Diamondbacks and Rays joined the majors.

Yet, paradoxically, they're down.

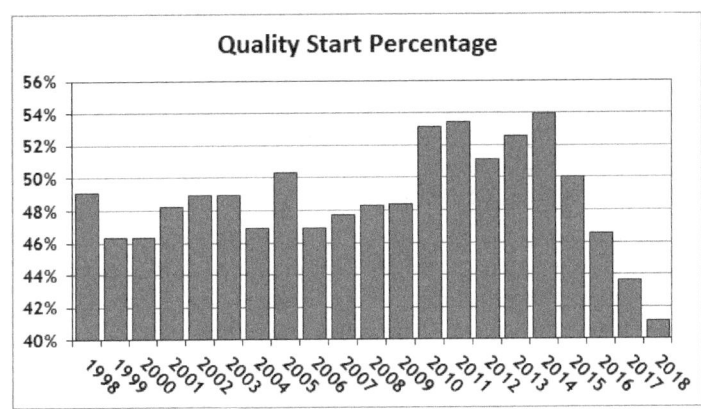

This graph covers only the 30-team era. In my article last week, though, I looked at the years 1908-2018. The result was the same. The 41 percent of starts in 2018 that were quality starts are an all-time low, well below the runners-up: 1930's 43 percent (the year teams scored an all-time record 5.55 runs per game) and last year's 44 percent.

The normal explanation for a dip in quality start percentage is an increase in scoring. When teams score a lot of runs, it's harder for starting pitchers to last six or more innings and limit opponents to three earned runs. From 1998 to 2014, the correlation between runs scored per game and the percentage of starts that were quality starts was -0.94. That means there was an extremely close relationship: More runs, fewer quality starts. Too small a sample? Go back to the start of the Expansion Era, 1961, and the relationship is even more negative, a -0.95 correlation, though 2014.

But that's broken down over the past four years:

- 2015: Runs per game increased from 4.07 to 4.25, quality start percentage decreased from 54.0 to 50.1. Yes, that's a negative relationship, but the regression model would predict a decline of 1.5 percentage points. We got 3.9 instead.
- 2016: Runs per game increased from 4.25 to 4.48, quality start percentage decreased from 50.1 to 46.6. Past experience would suggest a decline of just 1.8 percentage points. We got 3.4.
- 2017: Runs per game increased from 4.48 to 4.65, quality start percentage decreased from 46.6 to 43.6. Again, the direction's right, but the magnitude isn't. Using the relationship from 1998 to 2014, that increase in scoring should've reduced quality starts by 1.3 percentage points, not 2.9.
- 2018: Runs per game declined from 4.65 to 4.45. That should've resulted in the quality start percentage moving in the other direction, rising 1.6 points. It didn't. It fell 2.6 points, as noted, to an all-time low.

Granted, we're talking about just four years here. Maybe they're outliers. But I don't think they are. Quality starts, as noted, are as good or better than ever. But they're rarer than ever as well. And I think I know why.

To get a quality start, you need to allow three or fewer earned and pitch at least six innings. That's 18 outs. Here's a graph showing the number of starting pitchers who limited their opponents to three or fewer earned runs but got pulled after pitching at least five innings but fewer than six:

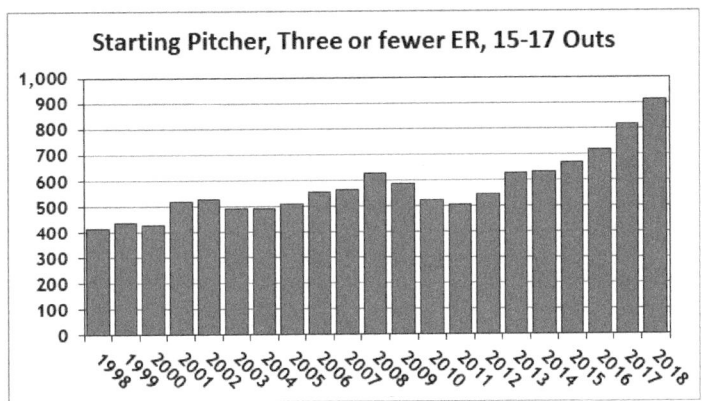

A pitcher getting 15 outs pitched five innings. A pitcher getting 16 outs pitched 5 1/3. A pitcher getting 17 outs pitched 5 2/3. More than ever before, pitchers are being removed from games in which they are within 1-3 outs of a quality start, falling just short of the six-inning finish line. Widespread acknowledgement of the times-through-the-order penalty and a flotilla of available bullpen arms is making the quality start simultaneously both more excellent and more rare.

Which is ironic, given that we saw a new post-war quality start record this season:

Rank	Pitcher	Season	Consecutive QS
1	Jacob deGrom	2018	24
2	Bob Gibson	1968	22
-	Chris Carpenter	2005	22
4	Johan Santana	2004	21
5	Luis Tiant	1968	20
-	Mike Scott	1986	20
-	Jake Arrieta	2015	20
8	Robin Roberts	1952	19
-	Tom Seaver	1973	19
-	Jack Morris	1983	19
-	Greg Maddux	1998	19
-	Josh Johnson	2010	19
-	Jon Lester	2014	19

While there have been longer streaks spread over multiple seasons, no pitcher since World War II threw more consecutive quality starts in one year than Jacob deGrom this year. The fact that he did in a year in which quality starts were the rarest they've ever been adds to the accomplishment.

—*Rob Mains is an author of Baseball Prospectus.*

Heads-Up Hacking—The First Pitch

Matthew Trueblood

Batters fell behind in a higher percentage of all plate appearances in 2018 than in any previous season for which we have pitch-by-pitch data. That kind of granular information goes back only to 1988, but we might safely assume (given all we know about baseball as it had been before that, and as it has been in the years since) that batters have *never* fallen behind at a higher rate than they did last season.

Through the 1990s, the percentage of all plate appearances that began 0-1 hovered in the high 30s and low 40s. In the 2000s, it rose steadily but slowly, through the mid-40s. In 2018, 49.8 percent of all trips to the plate began 0-1. That, as much as anything, captures in microcosm the nature of hitting in MLB today.

A countdown clock toward strike three begins ticking almost the moment a batter takes his place in the box. The league's adjusted OPS+ on the first pitch was higher in 2018 than ever before, and that has been true in most of the last 10 seasons. Batters hit .264/.289/.442 in all plate appearances in which they swung at the first pitch last season, and .241/.330/.395 in all plate appearances in which they took that first offering.

The percentage differences in batting average and isolated power there favor swinging at the first pitch by more than in any season since 1988, while the difference in on-base percentage favors taking by more than ever. If you want to get on base at a decent clip, it's a good idea to be patient, but you run the risk of missing the only chances you'll get to produce power.

Milwaukee Brewers 2019

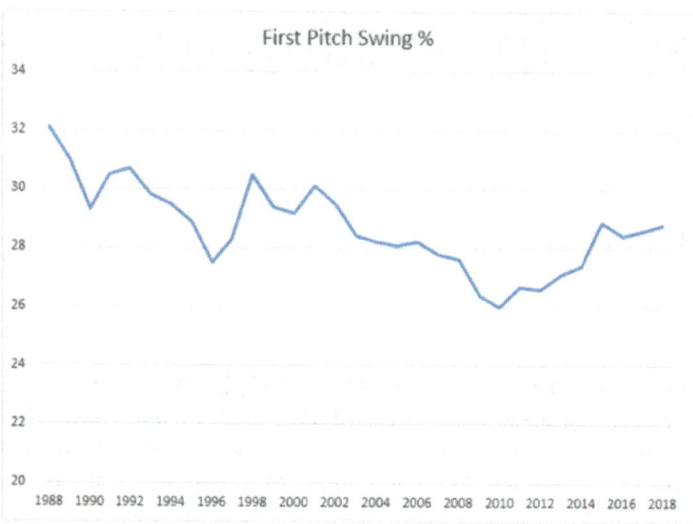

The league swung at the first pitch 28.8 percent of the time in 2018. With the isolated exception of 2015, that's the highest that number has climbed since 2002, but it might not be high enough. With the help of BP research maven Rob McQuown, I looked at the aggregate Called Strike Probability (CSProb) on the first pitch for each season since 2008, when the implementation of PITCHf/x first made measuring that possible. It's risen sharply during that period.

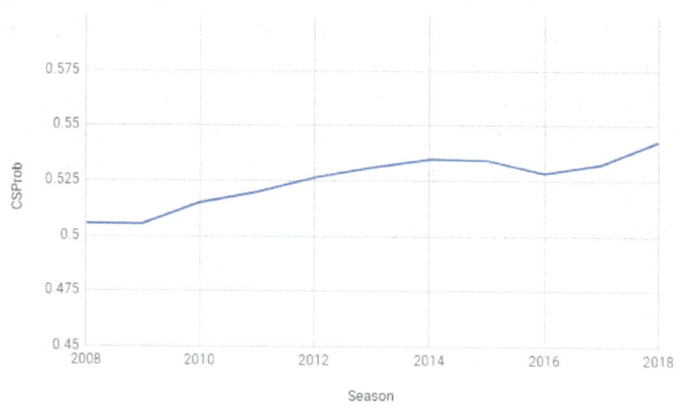

Called Strike Probability, First Pitch of PA (2008-2018)

Called Strike Probability is exactly what it sounds like: a pitch with a given CSProb has roughly that chance of being called a strike, if not swung at. In 2018, a batter who took 100 first pitches from a random sampling of the league's pitchers might expect to fall behind 54 or 55 times—up from 50 or 51 times in 2008. Almost regardless of pitch type (and, notably, especially in the case of fastballs), the first pitch tends to have more of the zone right now than ever before.

Pitchers are better at throwing strikes. They have better stuff, and believe more in their ability to miss bats within the zone. Perhaps most importantly, they know that batters are looking for one thing on the first pitch: a fastball. If they don't get it, they're likely to take the pitch. Check out how the use of sinkers and four-seamers on the first pitch has changed in a decade:

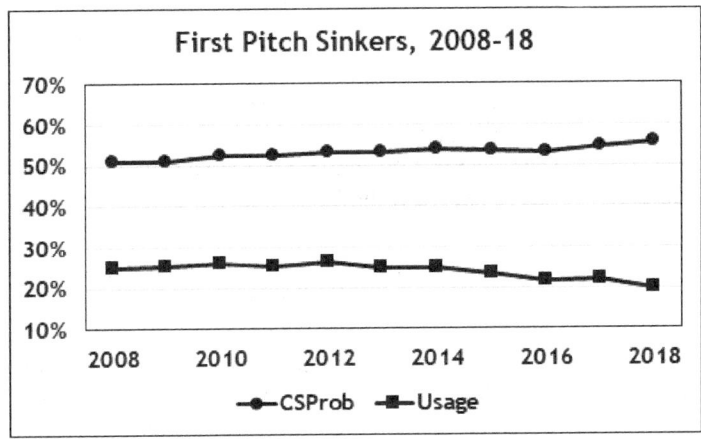

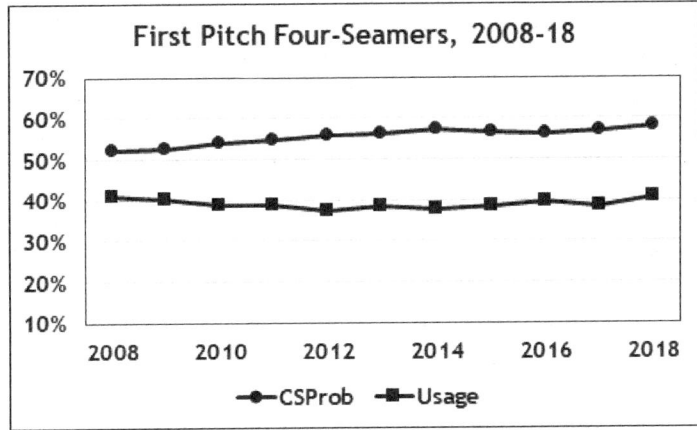

The sinker is losing its place in baseball, but the rate at which pitchers have thrown it on the first pitch hasn't dropped any faster than its usage rate in other counts. Pitchers have actually gone to their four-seamer *more* often to open counts, in the last few years, after a dip in the 2012-2015 period. What's really changed, though, and what shows up in both charts above, is that pitchers are catching more of the zone with first-pitch fastballs than they were a decade ago, or a half-decade ago. They're attacking right away, even with the pitch they know batters are expecting. The message is pretty clear: batters are being too passive.

Sliders, curves, and changeups each have more of the zone when thrown on the first pitch than they did several years ago, too, though the effect is less pronounced. Pitchers have seen the numbers; they know batters are doing better on the first pitch itself. They still feel safe throwing more and better strikes than ever before, figuring they'll come out ahead as long as they keep getting ahead to open each battle.

The Moneyball revolution brought an increased league-wide focus on OBP, which resulted in a de facto mandate to take a more patient tack at the plate. It worked very well for a while, as batters with poor plate discipline were compelled to either adjust or be expelled from the league, and pitchers with poor control were slowly weeded out.

However, concurrent with that revolution, and spurred by it in some ways, was the evolution of the pitching paradigm that now dominates the game. As batters ratcheted up their focus on inflating pitch counts and working walks, pitchers honed theirs on throwing strikes and missing bats. The league's understanding of what makes a good pitcher improved at least as much, from the mid-1990s through the mid-2000s, as its understanding of what makes a good hitter. As amphetamines and other performance-enhancing drugs were phased mostly out of the game, and as PITCHf/x broke onto the scene, individuals and teams learned how to exploit the evolved approaches of even the smartest hitters.

The ability to avoid making outs is still the most valuable one in baseball, but the magnitude of its eclipse of slugging is smaller than ever. To a greater extent than power, on-base skills derive their value from chaining—from the on-base skill levels of the players on either side of a given individual. Eleven years ago, when the housing crisis hit, people learned the hard way that the value of their homes depended a good deal on the values of their neighbors' homes. The same wasn't true, though, of their cars. So it is now, with OBP and SLG.

The global OBP in 2018 was .318. The only seasons since the Dead Ball Era in which the league got on base at a worse clip were 2013-2015, 1988, 1971-1972, and 1963-1968. This is all happening despite the aforementioned evolution of the science of hitting. It's happening despite a shift in approach and focus, one that would steer OBP ever higher, if only it were working.

Instead, it's sitting at a low ebb, and while it does so, even guys who get on base often are a little less helpful than they were 10 years ago—or 20, or 40, or 60, or 70, or 80, or 90. They're less helpful, that is, because unless there happen to be three or four other guys in the lineup who get on just as regularly, their contribution is merely to forestall the inevitable. Runs happen, increasingly, when a sudden bang happens, and that means attacking early in the count—because pitchers are sure as hell doing that.

In a league making contact on barely 75 percent of its swings, and a league in which an increasing number of pitchers can throw multiple off-speed pitches for strikes in any count, the only way to consistently generate offense is going to be aggressive. This isn't necessarily true for individuals, like Mookie Betts and Jose Ramirez, who make a lot of contact and have excellent plate discipline, and whose power comes from such natural quickness in a short stroke. Most players have to make tradeoffs, though, whether it be lowering their contact rate or raising their chase rate, in order to consistently make the quality of contact necessary to survive in today's game.

Highest %	Lowest %
Javier Baez – 48.3	Joe Mauer – 4.6
Freddie Freeman – 47.1	Mookie Betts – 9.7
Ozzie Albies – 46.3	Brett Gardner – 10.7
Jose Altuve – 44.2	Jose Ramirez – 12.0
Nick Castellanos – 44.1	Jason Kipnis – 13.8
Joey Gallo – 42.3	Jesus Aguilar – 14.5
Corey Dickerson – 40.9	Xander Bogaerts – 15.8
Salvador Perez – 40.8	Brian Dozier – 16.3
Eddie Rosario – 40.7	Mike Trout – 17.6
Nick Ahmed – 40.4	Yasmani Grandal – 17.6

Top 10 and Bottom 10 Hitters, First-Pitch Swing Rate (2018)

The question isn't which of these lists one prefers, but what they each convey, qualitatively, about the cat-and-mouse game of early-count hitting. Those top five on the left, especially, drive home the fact that for most players, getting aggressive early in the count is now key to keeping strikeout rate down and hitting for power.

For now, the message is: pitchers are coming right after batters with the nastiest stuff they've ever had. Batters had better stop giving away strike one and force hurlers to adjust, or the global OBP crisis is only going to get worse.

—*Matthew Trueblood is an author of Baseball Prospectus.*

A Hymn for the Index Stat

Patrick Dubuque

We survived without computers. I know this, because I remember the day when my dad hooked up his brand-new Atari 400 computer to the back of our 12-inch Magnavox television, and the perfect blue of the memo pad lit up for the first time. I was born just on the edge of that transitional generation, of learning cursive and balancing checkbooks and just doing math all the time, constant manual arithmetic.

It still amazes me. We learned how to sail ships without computers. We learned how to do calculus. We built towers that didn't fall down, most of the time. We engineered catapults to knock them down anyway. We built a robust system of philosophy called "utilitarianism," founded on the principle that the good of an action is evaluated by summing the effects of that action, which is the kind of formula that would make the world's mainframes crash. The whole foundation of statistics as a field is "here's math you could easily do but would die of old age first."

The fact of the matter is that there is too much math in the world to do. There are too many things changing, and too many things too small to notice, for us to handle. At some point, they become too much for the computers to handle as well, which is why we have chaos theory and undetectable earthquakes, but it's not an even fight. At some point, we fall back on intuition, and given how under-equipped we are, we're forced to bestow that intuition with some sort of supernatural superiority, the "gut feeling," that we can't prove because we can only intuit that our intuition is better.

We're all lousy at intuition, and wonderful at lying to ourselves about it. The honest truth is that computers are far better at intuition than we are, because in order to know what feels "off" you have to know what's "on." In order to do that you have to constantly reassess the average of everything, then re-rank your own experience against it.

Test your own, by comparing these three anonymous lines:

Player	G	HR	AVG	OBP	SLG
Player A	156	38	.259	.342	.535
Player B	154	38	.280	.348	.527
Player C	158	38	.266	.343	.509

These all seem like pretty similar players, right? The second one a touch more batted-ball dependent, the third a little less strong, but all pretty good hitters. And you'd be right, about the latter. Not the former.

Here's the breakdown:

- Player A: 1991 Howard Johnson, 141 DRC+
- Player B: 1996 Dean Palmer, 121 DRC+
- Player C: 2018 Giancarlo Stanton, 114 DRC+

Baseball is fortunate to have escaped the seismic shifts of so many other sports, where the talents and performances of other eras are nearly unrecognizable. (And not just other sports: try to explain the greatness of the movie Duck Soup without adjusting for era.) But they're still there, and they're nearly impossible to account for manually, without having to resort to sweeping generalizations like "steroid era" or juiced-ball era" to throw out entire swathes of production.

This is all to say that we should celebrate the index stat, that simple 100-based scale with such a humble aim: just to give context. It's hard to imagine how we lived without them for so long. Sabermetricians have always tried to make their stats look like other stats: True Average mapped to batting average, FIP molded to look like and compare to ERA. It's easy to understand the motivation—these statistics carry an emotional value in them that is hard to resist, as with the .300 hitter and the 2.00 ERA—but even they fall prey to the same loss of scale as their unadjusted counterparts. If a .300 average means different things in different years, does that hold true for a .300 True Average?

Instead, 100 doesn't say anything, except above average or below. And it does it instantly, for every season in every run environment for any statistic we want it to. We should have more index stats: K%+, so we can stop comparing Mike Clevinger's career 9.46 K/9 to Nolan Ryan's 9.55. HBP%+, so we can note that Ron Hunt was getting plunked when nobody else was getting plunked, as opposed to that imitator Brandon Guyer. Some might note how stale these references are and accuse league-adjustment as a backward-looking drive, and this is true. But we're always looking backward, always comparing the new with the expectations already set. The index stat just forces us to be honest.

There's always resistance to a new statistic, especially one so outwardly simple and so internally complex. We tend to stick with what we know, even in the case of formulas that are supposed to tell us what we know. But if your resistance is that it seems too complicated, too counterintuitive, too "black boxy," I encourage you to consider why you feel that way. Because the real world is infinitely more complicated than baseball, where all the pitches go in one basic direction and the baserunners are only allowed to travel in four directions. Baseball statistics based on mixed methodology are almost impossibly intricate. So are skyscrapers and automobiles. That's why we have computers—to take the guesswork out of them.

—*Patrick Dubuque is an author of Baseball Prospectus.*

Index of Names

Aguilar, Jesus	20	Jeffress, Jeremy	62
Albers, Matt	96	Knebel, Corey	64
Anderson, Chase	46	Kratz, Erik	95
Arcia, Orlando	22	Lutz, Tristen	81, 100
Ashby, Aaron	96	Moustakas, Mike	32
Barker, Luke	87	Nelson, Jimmy	92
Barnes, Jacob	96	Nottingham, Jacob	82
Braun, Ryan	24	Olczak, Jon	96
Brown, Zack	88, 100	Peralta, Freddy	66
Burnes, Corbin	48	Perez, Hernan	34
Cain, Lorenzo	26	Petricka, Jake	68
Chacin, Jhoulys	50	Pina, Manny	36
Claudio, Alex	52	Ponce, Cody	93
Davies, Zach	54	Ray, Corey	83, 101
Derby, Bubba	89	Rojas, Robie	95
Diplan, Marcos	90	Saladino, Tyler	95
Dubon, Mauricio	78, 102	Sanchez, Miguel	96
Erceg, Lucas	104	Shaw, Travis	38
Ernesto, Larry	95	Smith, Burch	70
Feliciano, Mario	103	Spangenberg, Cory	40
Gamel, Ben	28	Stokes, Troy	84, 103
Gatewood, Jake	79	Supak, Trey	94
Gonzalez, Luis	96	Suter, Brent	72
Grandal, Yasmani	30	Taylor, Tyrone	95
Gray, Joe	103	Thames, Eric	42
Grisham, Trent	95	Tomlin, Josh	74
Guerra, Junior	56	Torres-Costa, Quintin	96
Hader, Josh	58	Turang, Brice	85, 101
Hiura, Keston	80, 99	Wahl, Bobby	96
Houser, Adrian	60	Wilkerson, Aaron	96
Jankins, Thomas	91	Williams, Taylor	96

Milwaukee Brewers 2019

Wilson, Weston 86
Woodruff, Brandon 76
Yelich, Christian 44

Ballpark diagrams for Baseball Prospectus are created by THIRTY81Project, a design concept offering original ballpark artwork, including the new 'Ballparks of 2019' 11 x 17 color print.

Visit **www.thirty81project.com** for full details.